origami
Monsters & Magic

Isamu Sasagawa

TUTTLE Publishing

Tokyo | Rutland, Vermont | Singapore

Introduction

Welcome to the magical world of origami!

When you turn the pages of this book, a lot of origami of monsters and magic will be revealed to you.

Keep tackling and clearing each one, and at the end, face the most difficult final monster, the Infernal Dragon!

Once you've folded that, there is a treasure chest waiting for you as a reward!

Let's start an origami adventure that becomes more and more fun as you fold the objects!

— **Isamu Sasagawa**

Let's go on an adventure together!

Oriko

She is a hard worker, but sometimes she's a bit clumsy. She loves to eat, and even the monsters look delicious to her.

Gamio

He is gentle and kind, but a bit cowardly. He wants to get strong through his quests and defeat the monsters.

Chapter 1

Defeat the Monsters!

LOST IN THE MAGICAL FOREST

Chapter 2

Add Strength Points with Magic Items!

TRAINING AT THE SCHOOL OF MAGIC

Chapter 4

Test Your Improved Mettle!

MIDNIGHT DUEL IN THE CEMETERY

Chapter 3

Power Up with a Sword and Shield!

GETTING EQUIPPED IN THE WEAPON SHOP

Chapter 5
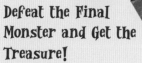

Defeat the Final Monster and Get the Treasure!

SHOWDOWN IN THE DUNGEON

GOAL!

How to View the Video Lessons

To access the how-to videos

1. Make sure you have an Internet connection.
2. Type the URL below into your web browser.

tuttlepublishing.com/origami-monsters-and-magic

For support, you can email us at info@tuttlepublishing.com

Evil Tree Stump

It pretends to be an ordinary tree stump, but then it startles anyone who sits on it. It may also chase after travelers.

		VIDEO
Attack Power	★★	Type this URL into your browser: tuttlepublishing.com/origami-monsters-and-magic
Defense Power	★★★★	
Magic Power	★★★★★	
Special Abilities	Misleads people with magic Runs fast	

Basic Shape — Fold a 16-row fold (see Page 125)

Enchanted Island Map

Origami Adventure Awaits!

School of Magic

Magical Forest

Dungeon

Weapon
Shop

Cemetery

TABLE OF CONTENTS

Introduction 2

Enchanted Island Map 4

Basic Folds and Symbols 10

1 LOST IN THE MAGICAL FOREST

Evil Tree Stump 14

Bewitched Wolf 16

Tornado Rabbit 18

Pecking Bird 20

Toxic Mushrooms 21

Forest Gnomes 22

The Werebear 24

Fish Bones 28

Shellfish of Terror 30

Prehistoric Fish 32

The Loch Ness Monster 34

2 TRAINING AT THE SCHOOL OF MAGIC

The Magician's Hat 38

Magic Wand 40

Magic Lamp 42

Riding Broom 44

Messenger Owl 45

Cat Familiar 46

Mandrake 48

Unicorn 50

Phoenix 52

3 GETTING EQUIPPED IN THE WEAPON SHOP

Flexible Sword 60

Bolt Thrower 62

Self-Destruct Button 64

War Hammer 66

Ninja Star 68

Battle Claws 70

Invincible Shield 72

4 MIDNIGHT DUEL IN THE CEMETERY

Lantern Ghost 74

Noodle-Necked Monster 76

The "Disappearing" Ghost 78

Tombstone 80

Jaw-Dropping Skull 82

Wobbly Zombie 84

The Grim Reaper 86

Reaper's Scythe 88

Squawking Crow 89

The Face of Dracula 90

Crucifix 92

TRY USING THE MAGIC YOU'VE LEARNED

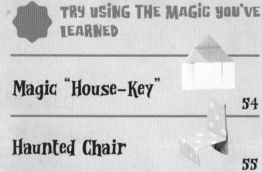

Magic "House-Key" 54

Haunted Chair 55

Magic Soft Serve Ice Cream Cone 56

GAG NOVELTIES FROM THE MAGIC SHOP

Pop-Out Eyeballs 94

Fake Moustache 96

Wagging Tongue 98

SHOWDOWN IN THE DUNGEON

Creepy Hands 102

Chattering Teeth 104

Flaming Torch 106

Flapping Bat 108

Whispering Imp 110

Deadly Spider 111

Infernal Dragon 112

Treasure Chest 116

Gemstones 118

Achievement Checklist 120

Origami Bases

Blintz Base 123

Boat Base 123

8-Row Precrease (1) 124

8-Row Precrease (2) 124

16-Row Precrease 125

Fish Base 126

Balloon Base 126

Crane Base 127

How to Use Round Stickers!

This book contains lots of monsters with eyes and mouths. If you use round stickers that are available at craft or office supply shops as well as dollar stores, you can make eyes and mouths easily. You can cut them in half to make slanted eyes, or layer two stickers of different sizes together and so on to make fun faces. You can also draw on the eyes and mouths instead, of course!

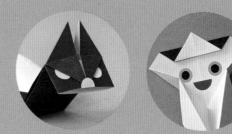

Basic Folds and Symbols

The folding diagrams that are used to describe how objects are folded have various symbols on them. If you memorize them, folding origami becomes easy.

Valley Fold

Fold the paper so that the dashed line become a "valley."

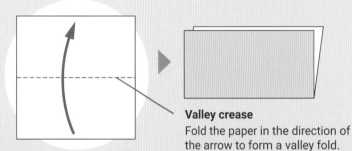

Valley crease
Fold the paper in the direction of the arrow to form a valley fold.

Mountain Fold

Fold the paper at the dashed line so that the paper becomes a "mountain" toward the outside.

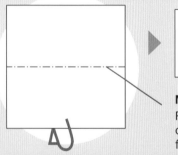

Mountain crease
Fold the paper in the direction of the arrow to form a mountain fold.

Press Firmly With Your Fingers Like an Iron!

Press and slide your fingers firmly along creases as if you were ironing them. This way, the creases will be sharp and straight.

Press and Slide!

Make a Crease

If you fold the paper once and then open it up again, a crease is made that become a guideline for the next fold.

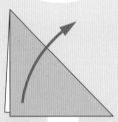

1 After making an valley fold in the direction of the arrow, unfold the paper to return it to its original state.

2 A crease has formed where you folded.

Open Up and Flatten

■ Open Up a Square and Flatten

Place a finger into the square pocket indicated by the squat up arrow ⬆. Then, open up the paper in the direction of the long arrow and flatten.

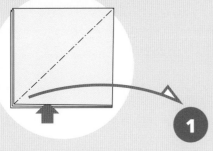

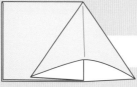

1 A finger has been inserted into the square pocket and the pocket has been opened up.

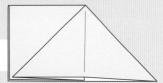

2 Flatten the pocket and it transforms into a triangle!

▲ Open Up a Triangle and Flatten

Place your fingers in the triangular pocket indicated by the squat up arrow ⬆. Then, open up the paper in the direction of the long arrow and flatten.

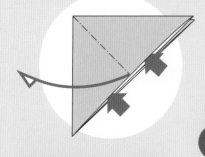

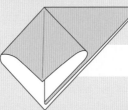

1 Fingers have been inserted into the triangular pocket and the pocket has been opened up.

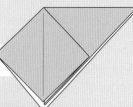

2 Flatten the pocket and it transforms into a square!

Stepped Folds

Make a mountain fold and a valley fold next to each other so that the folds form a "step."

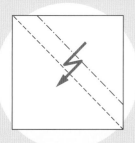

1 After having folded the paper in half with a valley fold first, fold the paper back at the dashed line.

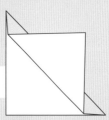

2 The mountain fold and the valley fold are next to each other to form a "step."

Make Horns

Make points like horns at the corners indicated with double arrows ⋀.

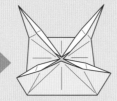

If you fold the paper in the direction of the arrows, "horns" (flaps) will be formed.

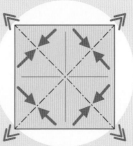

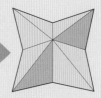

⋀ Pinch the double arrow corners to form "horns."

Inside Reverse Fold

Pop a folded corner inside out.

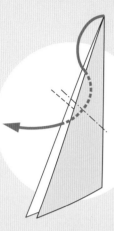

2 Open up the paper a little, and then fold the paper inward at the crease.

Press with your fingers to fold it in.

1 Make a fold at the dashed line and open it up again to make a crease.

3 Fold down more....

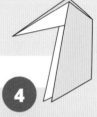

4 The inside reverse fold is done.

Outside Reverse Fold

Invert a corner to the outside along a crease.

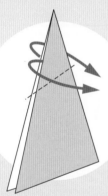

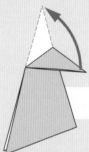

1 Make a fold at the dashed line and open it up again to make a crease.

2 Open up the first fold, and turn the paper over to the outside at the crease made in step 1.

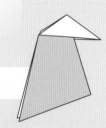

3 Once it's folded down, the outside reverse fold is complete.

Reorganize Layers

Expose a side of the paper that is different from the side you were folding.

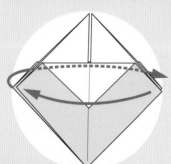

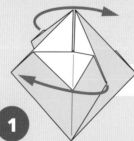

1 Fold the front side to the left, and the back side to the right.

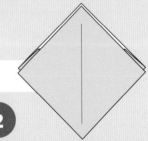

2 Different sides from the ones you were folding have been exposed.

1

LOST IN THE MAGICAL FOREST

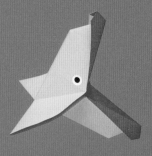

While we were searching for treasure, we got lost in a forest inhabited by lake and woodland monsters! Let's clear them out quickly to escape the forest as soon as we can!

Evil Tree Stump

This entity mimics an ordinary tree stump, but then it startles anyone who sits on it. It may also chase after travelers.

		VIDEO
Attack Power	★ ★	Type this URL into your browser: tuttlepublishing.com/ origami-monsters -and-magic
Defense Power	★ ★ ★ ★	
Magic Power	★ ★ ★ ★ ★	
Special Abilities	Misleads people with magic. Runs fast.	

Basic Shape — Fold a 16-Row Precrease (see page 125).

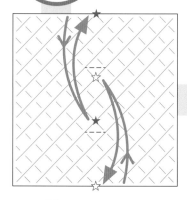

1 Open up the paper completely. Fold the red-star-marked points and the white-star-marked points together to make creases on one square each only along the dashed lines.

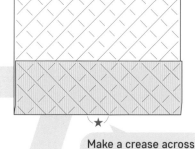

Make a crease across one square only.

Here, the lower side is being folded. Only crease along the part marked with a red star, and then unfold the paper.

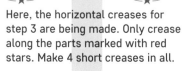

Here, the horizontal creases for step 3 are being made. Only crease along the parts marked with red stars. Make 4 short creases in all.

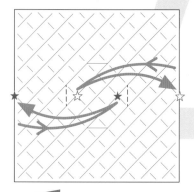

2 Fold the left and right sides in the same way as in step 1.

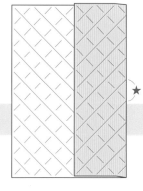

Here, the right side is being folded. Only crease along the part marked with a red star. Unfold the paper.

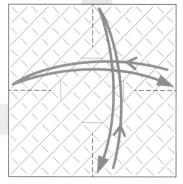

3 Fold vertically and horizontally along the dashed lines to make 4 short creases.

In the corresponding video, this is titled "Evil Stump."

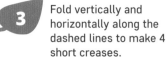

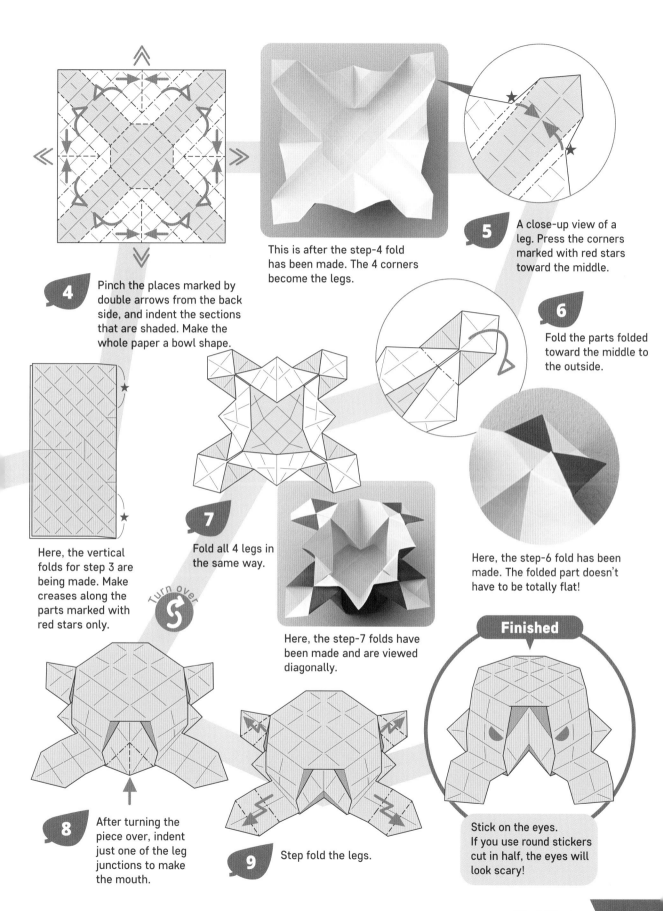

4 Pinch the places marked by double arrows from the back side, and indent the sections that are shaded. Make the whole paper a bowl shape.

This is after the step-4 fold has been made. The 4 corners become the legs.

5 A close-up view of a leg. Press the corners marked with red stars toward the middle.

6 Fold the parts folded toward the middle to the outside.

Here, the vertical folds for step 3 are being made. Make creases along the parts marked with red stars only.

Turn over **S**

7 Fold all 4 legs in the same way.

Here, the step-6 fold has been made. The folded part doesn't have to be totally flat!

Here, the step-7 folds have been made and are viewed diagonally.

Finished

8 After turning the piece over, indent just one of the leg junctions to make the mouth.

9 Step fold the legs.

Stick on the eyes. If you use round stickers cut in half, the eyes will look scary!

Bewitched Wolf

This wolf appears suddenly in the dark and frightens people. It will pounce at you, so it's quite scary.

Attack Power	★ ★ ★
Defense Power	★ ★
Magic Power	★ ★ ★
Special Abilities	Crouches and pounces.

VIDEO
Type this URL into your browser:
tuttlepublishing.com/origami-monsters-and-magic

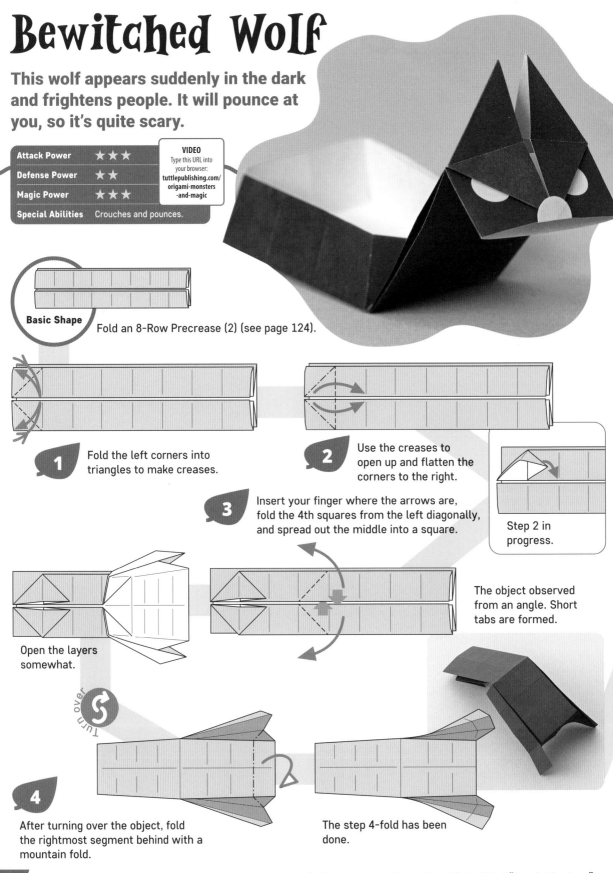

Basic Shape Fold an 8-Row Precrease (2) (see page 124).

1 Fold the left corners into triangles to make creases.

2 Use the creases to open up and flatten the corners to the right.

Step 2 in progress.

3 Insert your finger where the arrows are, fold the 4th squares from the left diagonally, and spread out the middle into a square.

Open the layers somewhat.

The object observed from an angle. Short tabs are formed.

Turn over

4 After turning over the object, fold the rightmost segment behind with a mountain fold.

The step 4-fold has been done.

In the corresponding video, this is titled "Dog in the Box."

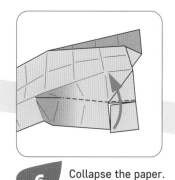

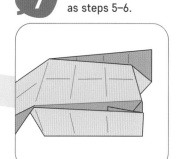

7
Step 6 is complete. Fold the opposite tab in the same way as steps 5–6.

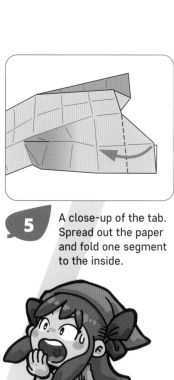

5
A close-up of the tab. Spread out the paper and fold one segment to the inside.

6
Collapse the paper.

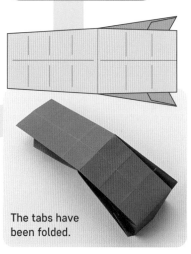

The tabs have been folded.

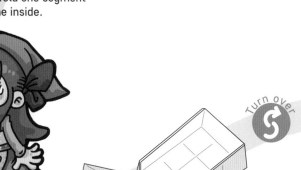

Turn over

8
The paper has been turned over. The body is in a box shape.

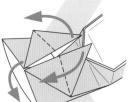

9
Stand up the ears, and swing down the face a bit.

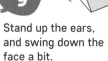

Finished

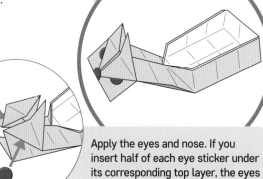

Apply the eyes and nose. If you insert half of each eye sticker under its corresponding top layer, the eyes will look menacing. Stick on the nose at the edge of the paper and fold half of it around to the back.

Grrrr GROWL!

If you push the upper body into the box and then loosen the hold on the box, the wolf face will spring out!

Tornado Rabbit

This rabbit spins like a tornado as it jumps and attacks. Don't be fooled by its cute appearance!

Attack Power	★ ★	
Defense Power	★	
Magic Power	★ ★	
Special Abilities	Twisting jump. It likes to trick people.	

VIDEO
Type this URL into your browser:
tuttlepublishing.com/ origami-monsters -and-magic

Basic Shape Fold an 8-Row Precrease (1) (see page 124) so that the white side of the paper faces outward.

Turn over

1 After turning the object over, fold diagonally both ways, and make X-shaped creases in the middle 4 squares (indicated in gray).

If you fold it like this, the X-shaped creases will be made.

2 Make X-shaped creases in the same way on the left and right 4 squares.

3 Fold and squeeze in the paper from the outside (as indicated by the arrows) to indent the X part.

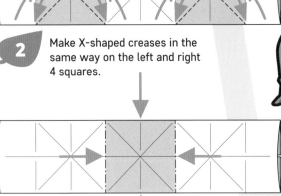

Press in firmly. This will become the spring.

In the corresponding video, this is titled "Tornado Jump Rabbit."

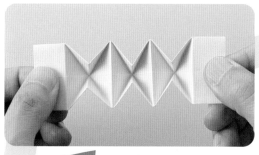

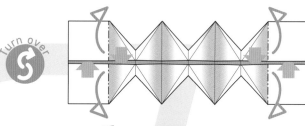

Turn over

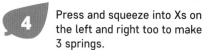

4 Press and squeeze into Xs on the left and right too to make 3 springs.

5 After turning it over, insert your fingers in the places indicated with squat arrows to form boxes on both sides.

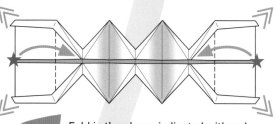

6 Fold in the places indicated with red stars, and point the corners marked with double arrows.

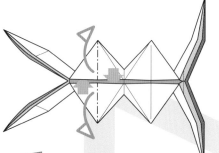

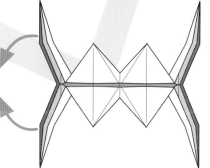

8 Insert your fingers inside the spring to form the mouth.

7 Fold up the left side only to form the ears.

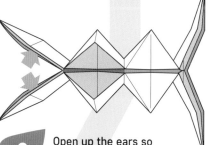

9 Open up the ears so that you can see the color inside.

Rotate

Finished

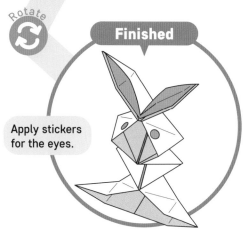

Apply stickers for the eyes.

Tornado Jump!

Slide the fingers you are using to hold down the bases of the ears as if you were scratching the rabbit. It will spring up! If you hold down beside just one ear, it will jump to the side.

Pecking Bird

A scary bird that pecks relentlessly with its sharp beak. ...Ouch, ouch!

Attack Power	★ ★	
Defense Power	★	
Magic Power	★	
Special Abilities	Attacks by pecking with its beak.	

VIDEO
Type this URL into your browser:
tuttlepublishing.com/origami-monsters-and-magic

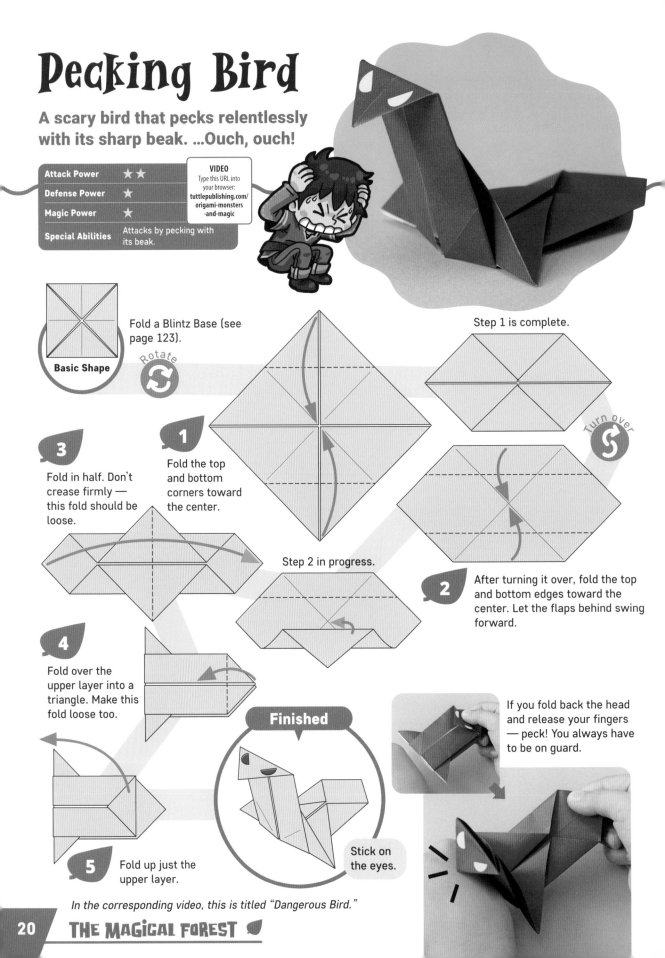

Basic Shape

Fold a Blintz Base (see page 123).

Rotate

Step 1 is complete.

Turn over

1 Fold the top and bottom corners toward the center.

Step 2 in progress.

2 After turning it over, fold the top and bottom edges toward the center. Let the flaps behind swing forward.

3 Fold in half. Don't crease firmly — this fold should be loose.

4 Fold over the upper layer into a triangle. Make this fold loose too.

Finished

Stick on the eyes.

If you fold back the head and release your fingers — peck! You always have to be on guard.

5 Fold up just the upper layer.

In the corresponding video, this is titled "Dangerous Bird."

Toxic Mushrooms

You may be fooled by their pretty appearance, and really want to eat them...but they are very poisonous!

Attack Power	★	
Defense Power	★ ★	
Magic Power	★ ★ ★	
Special Abilities	Alluring poisonous mushrooms	

VIDEO
Type this URL into your browser:
tuttlepublishing.com/origami-monsters-and-magic

Basic Shape Fold an 8-Row Precrease (1) (see page 124).

1 Open one row of square segments each up and down to make this shape. Fold up and down again to expose the white back side of the paper.

2 Fold the left 3 rows to the right.

Step 2 is complete.

Turn over

3 After turning the paper over top to bottom, fold the left corners into triangles to form creases.

4 Insert your fingers in the places indicated with squat arrows, and open up in the directions of the long arrows. Open up the edges toward the center.

Opening up the paper in step 4.

Step 4 is complete.

Rotate

Turn over

Finished

In the corresponding video, this is titled "Monster Mushroom."

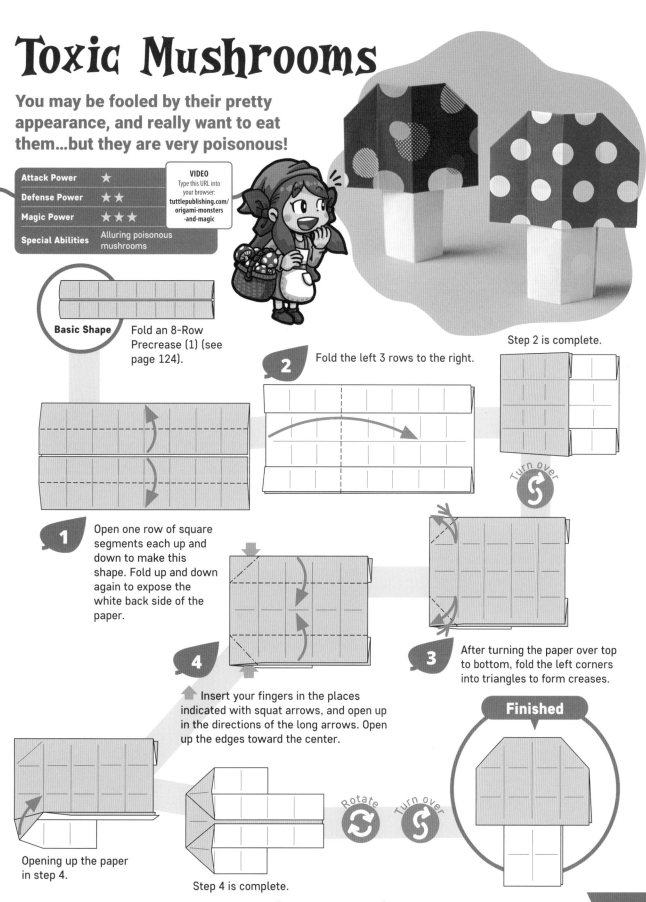

Forest Gnomes

If the tree branches sway and rustle even if there's no wind, that's probably the work of forest gnomes. They don't mean any harm.

Attack Power	None
Defense Power	★ ★
Magic Power	★ ★ ★
Special Abilities	They are mischievous but good natured.

VIDEO
Type this URL into your browser:
tuttlepublishing.com/origami-monsters-and-magic

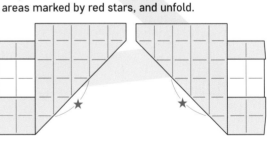

Basic Shape Fold an 8-Row Precrease (1) (see page 124).

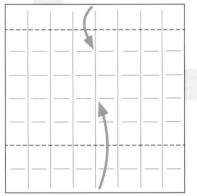

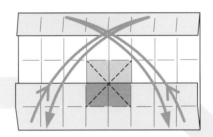

2

Fold diagonally twice, and make creases in the squares indicated with shading.

Step 2 is folded in this way. Make creases only in the areas marked by red stars, and unfold.

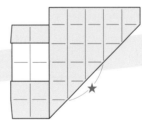

1

Open up the whole paper, and then fold down 1 row from the top and fold up 2 rows from the bottom.

Step 2 is complete.

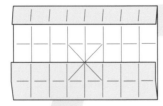

Turn over

3

After turning the piece over left to right, fold diagonally twice to make inverted V-shaped creases.

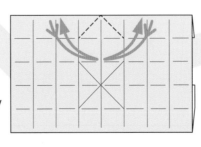

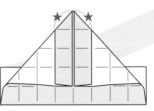

Step 3 in progress. Make creases only in the areas marked by red stars, and unfold.

In the corresponding video, this is titled "Forest Dwarf."

Step 3 is complete.

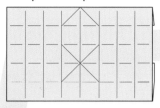

 Turn over

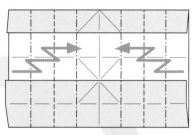

 4 After turning the piece over left to right, step fold in the left and right sides, leaving 2 columns in the middle.

 **6** Fold back the inverted V-shaped creases into a mountain fold.

 5 Push in both sides and indent the X part.

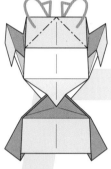

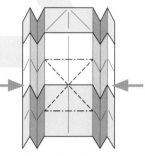

Here, the sides are being pushed in. This will become the neck.

 Turn over

Step 6 seen from the back. Leave the corner marked with a red star and fold in the other corners.

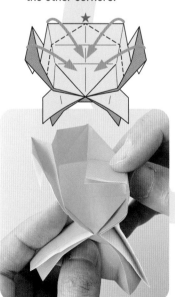

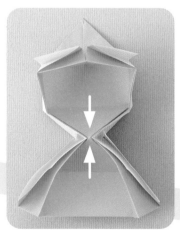

Finished

It's fun to make all kinds of faces!

 Turn over

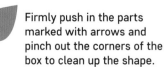 **7** Firmly push in the parts marked with arrows and pinch out the corners of the box to clean up the shape.

The Werebear

With its large paws and claws, the Werebear is the king of the forest who defeats his foes with one blow.
We pray that we don't encounter him....

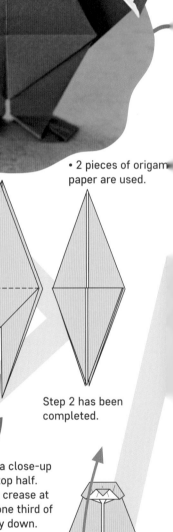

Attack Power	★★★★★
Defense Power	★★★★
Magic Power	★★★
Special Abilities	Supernatural strength. Its growl is frightening too.

VIDEO
Type this URL into your browser:
tuttlepublishing.com/origami-monsters-and-magic

This model is made in two parts

1 Body

• 2 pieces of origami paper are used.

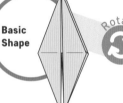

Basic Shape

Fold a Crane Base (see page 127).

Rotate

1
Once you have turned the piece over so that top is facing the bottom, fold the sides over to reorganize the layers.

2
Fold down the top flap.

Step 2 has been completed.

3
This is a close-up of the top half. Make a crease at about one third of the way down.

5
Fold the top down using the crease that you made in step 3. This will become the face.

Spread out both parts and do a mountain fold.

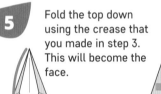

4
Insert your fingers where the squat arrows are, and spread open the paper.

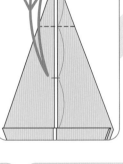

6
Fold up the corner.

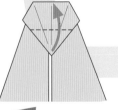

7
Fold down a small portion of the corner to make the nose.

The face is complete.

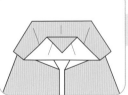

8
Return the triangle that you folded down in step 2 to the top.

In the corresponding video, this is titled "Bear King."

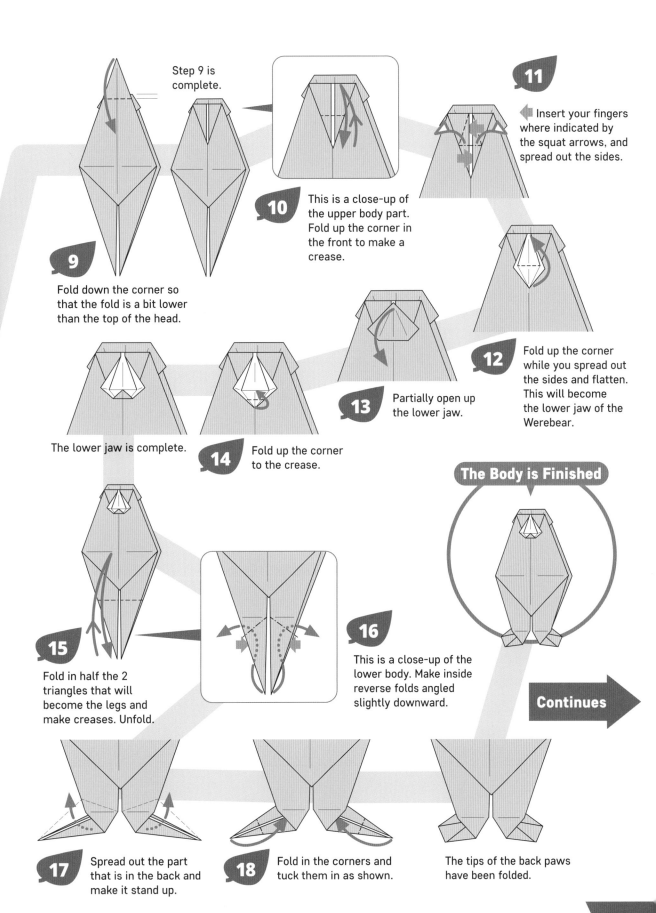

Step 9 is complete.

9 Fold down the corner so that the fold is a bit lower than the top of the head.

10 This is a close-up of the upper body part. Fold up the corner in the front to make a crease.

11 Insert your fingers where indicated by the squat arrows, and spread out the sides.

12 Fold up the corner while you spread out the sides and flatten. This will become the lower jaw of the Werebear.

13 Partially open up the lower jaw.

The lower jaw is complete.

14 Fold up the corner to the crease.

15 Fold in half the 2 triangles that will become the legs and make creases. Unfold.

16 This is a close-up of the lower body. Make inside reverse folds angled slightly downward.

The Body is Finished

Continues

17 Spread out the part that is in the back and make it stand up.

18 Fold in the corners and tuck them in as shown.

The tips of the back paws have been folded.

The Werebear

❷ Ears and Front Paws

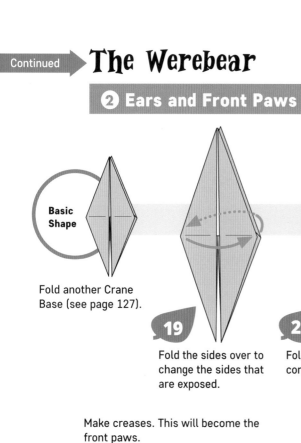

Basic Shape

Fold another Crane Base (see page 127).

19 Fold the sides over to change the sides that are exposed.

20 Fold up both bottom corners to the top.

21 Pull out the inside corners on the inside and slide them out to the bottom.

This shows the step-21 left side being pulled down. Hold onto the part marked with a red star and lower the corner. Pull the right side down and out in the same way.

Make creases. This will become the front paws.

22 Push the parts marked with red stars inside and fold them in. The left and right sides will open up and go up to meet the red dotted lines.

23

Spread out and do a mountain fold.

Make the ends of the paws stand up a bit.

24 This is a close-up of the tip of a paw. Insert your fingers where indicated by the squat arrows, spread out and squash flat.

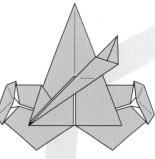

Step 26 is complete. The underlying flap is folded in the same way as in steps 25–26. This will become another ear.

25 Fold the top flap to the right diagonally. Make the angle align with the triangle inside (indicated by the dotted red line).

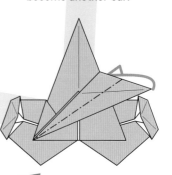

26 Fold half of the flap behind with a mountain fold.

The battle with the Evil Tree Stump has begun!

The ears and front paws are finished

27 Fold the tips of the ears behind with small mountain folds.

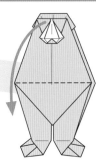

Put Parts 1 and 2 together!

28 Pull down the top flap of the Body part to the bottom.

29 Insert the ears and both front paws into the belly area.

30 Pull out the upper jaw over the ears.

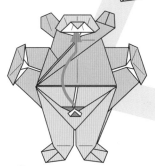

31 Fold up the lowered part of the body, and insert it under the upper jaw.

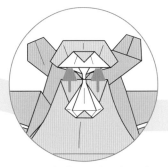

Insert the lower jaw into the pocket under the upper jaw.

Finished

Fish Bones

This fish doesn't have a transparent body so that you can see its bones — it only has bones! But it's still alive, which makes it creepy.

Attack Power	★ ★
Defense Power	★ ★ ★
Magic Power	★ ★
Special Abilities	Chomps on enemies, right down to the bones.

VIDEO
Type this URL into your browser:
tuttlepublishing.com/origami-monsters-and-magic

Basic Shape Fold a 16-Row Precrease (see page 125).

Turn over

1 After turning the piece over, make diagonal creases in the 3 places indicated.

Here, the creases are being made on the left. Make sure to make the crease only where marked by a red star.

2 This is a close-up of the left side. Pinch the squares next to the squares where you made the creases so that the middle (marked with a red star) becomes a mountain fold.

Turn over

Fold diagonally down, and make a crease only where marked by a red star. Make the other creases where indicated in the same way.

3 Spread out the area to the left of the red star into a square.

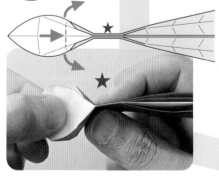

Pinch and hold the red-star part while you insert your fingers and spread out the part. Push your fingers into the corners to make a box shape.

4 Next, spread out the area to the right of the red star into a box shape. This is where you made the creases previously.

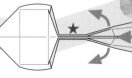

Pinch and hold onto the red-star part and push and squash firmly to the left.

In the corresponding video, this is titled "Boney Fish."

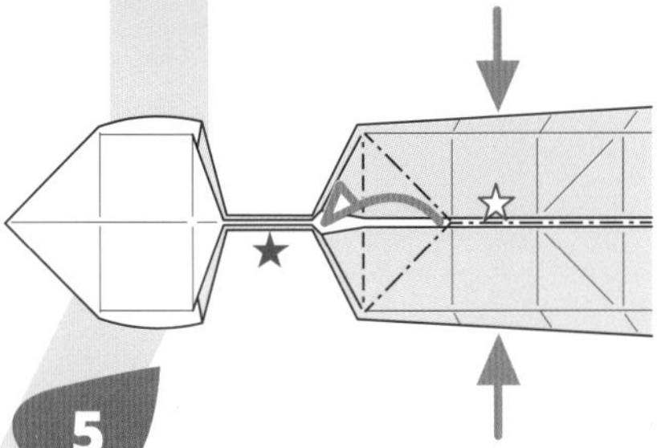

Push your pinched fingers firmly to the left and squash.

Step 5 is complete. A cross shape has been formed.

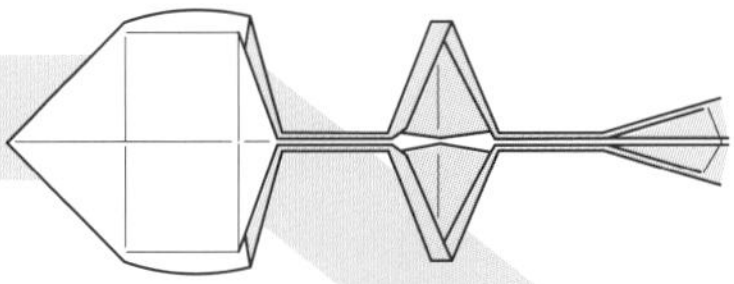

6 Repeat steps 4 and 5 for the creases to the right to form 2 more cross shapes.

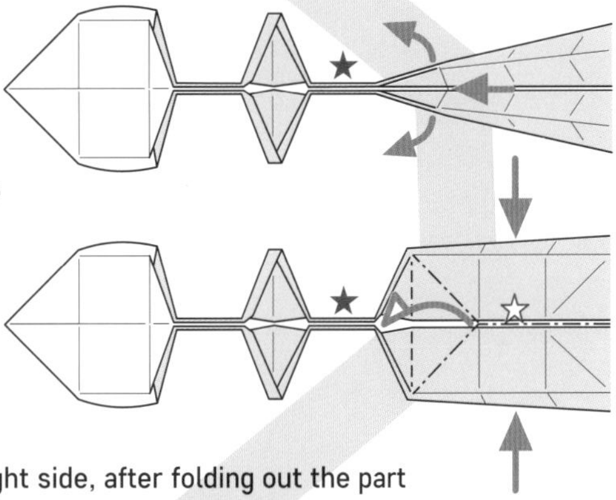

5 Press the square again where indicated by the blue arrows so that the middle (marked by a white star) becomes a mountain fold.

7 For the far right side, after folding out the part marked with a red star, spread out into a box shape as with the far left side.

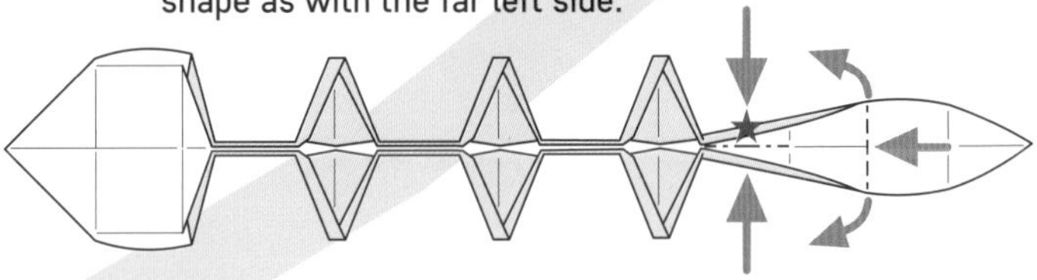

8 Fold in the end.

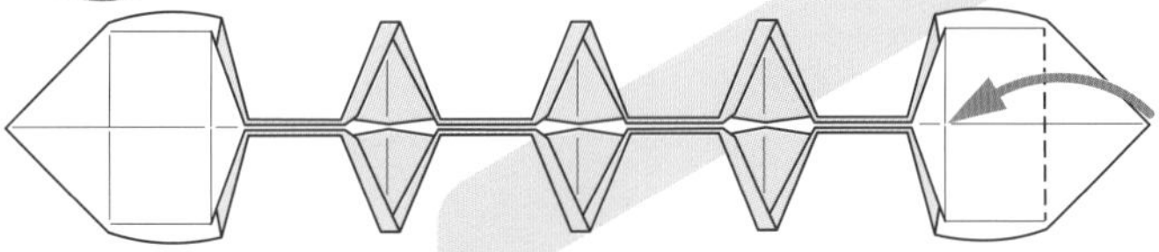

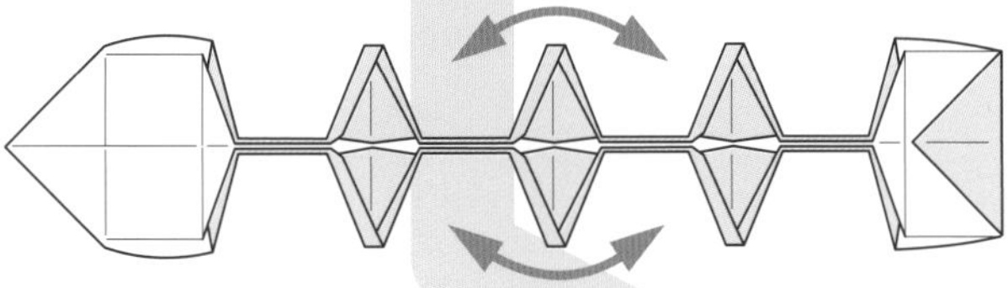

9 Bend the cross shapes this way and that and firmly sharpen the creases.

Turn over

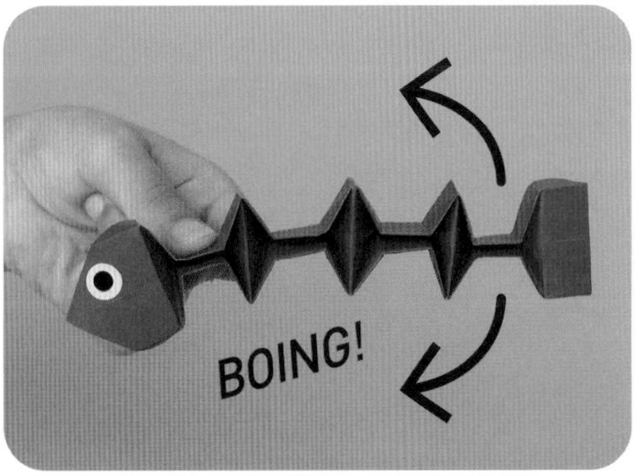

Shake the fish around while holding onto its neck. It will wobble like a spring!

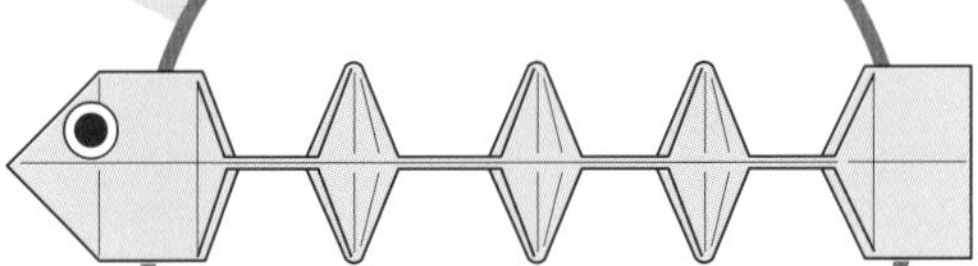

BOING!

Add stickers for eyes.

Finished

Shellfish of Terror

This shellfish lures people with its bright colors. Its favorite food is the fingers of humans. Once it clamps on, it doesn't let go.

Attack Power	★ ★
Defense Power	★ ★ ★ ★
Magic Power	★
Special Abilities	Although it looks beautiful, it is ferocious.

VIDEO
Type this URL into your browser:
tuttlepublishing.com/
origami-monsters
-and-magic

Basic Shape Fold an 8-Row Precrease (1) (see page 124).

1
Open up one row of square segments to the top and bottom to form this shape. Fold the 4 corners into triangles.

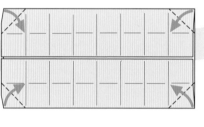

2 Fold in both corners of each triangle you folded in step 1 to make the form rounder.

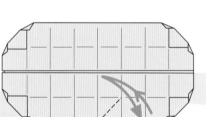

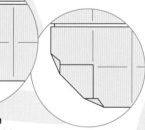

This is a close-up of the corners. Fold them back a little.

Step 2 is complete.

3
Make a crease next to the crease in the center as shown.

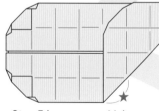

Step 3 in progress. Make a crease only where indicated by the red star. Unfold.

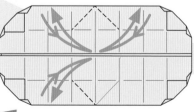

4 The crease (indicated by the red line) has been made. Make diagonal creases where indicated by dashed lines in the same way.

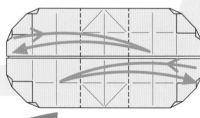

5 Fold firmly where indicated by dashed lines to make creases.

In the corresponding video, this is titled "Dangerous Shell."

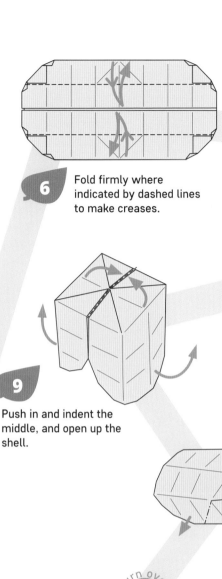

6 Fold firmly where indicated by dashed lines to make creases.

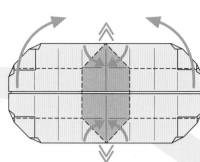

7 Fold in around the hexagon in the middle (the shaded area) to make points where indicated by double arrows. The left and right sides will stand up.

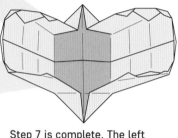

Step 7 is complete. The left and right sides are standing up. This will become the shell.

9 Push in and indent the middle, and open up the shell.

8 After you have turned the object over, fold in the triangles that are sticking out.

Put your finger straight into the opened shells.

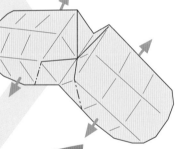

10 Fold the bases of the shell halves at the 4 places indicated by the arrows to refine the shell shapes.

11 After turning the object over, fold the middle securely.

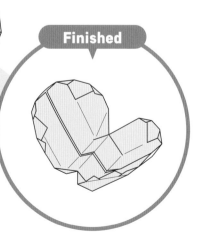

Finished

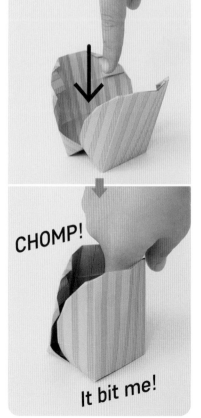

CHOMP!

It bit me!

Prehistoric Fish

This relic from the dinosaur age still lurks in the deep. It has a gaping maw with massive lips, and swallows its prey whole.

Attack Power	★ ★
Defense Power	★ ★
Magic Power	★ ★ ★
Special Abilities	Its mouth opens wider than its entire body is long!

VIDEO
Type this URL into your browser:
tuttlepublishing.com/origami-monsters-and-magic

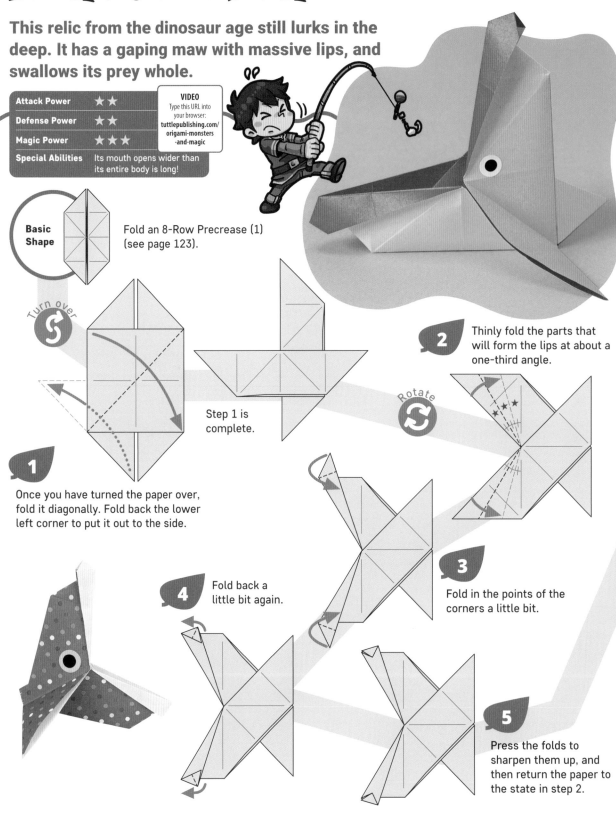

Basic Shape

Fold an 8-Row Precrease (1) (see page 123).

Turn over

1

Once you have turned the paper over, fold it diagonally. Fold back the lower left corner to put it out to the side.

Step 1 is complete.

Rotate

2

Thinly fold the parts that will form the lips at about a one-third angle.

3

Fold in the points of the corners a little bit.

4

Fold back a little bit again.

5

Press the folds to sharpen them up, and then return the paper to the state in step 2.

In the corresponding video, this is titled "Lip Fish."

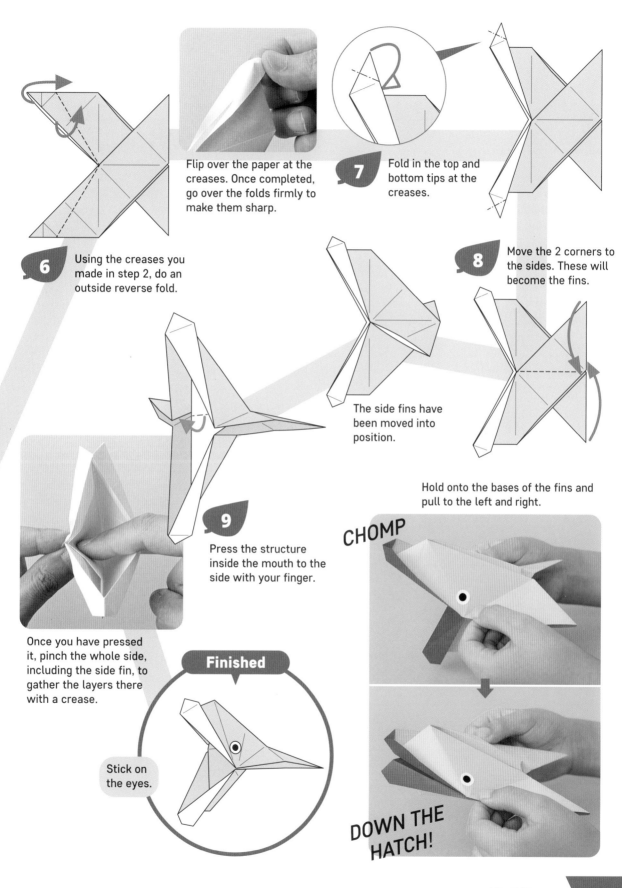

Flip over the paper at the creases. Once completed, go over the folds firmly to make them sharp.

7 Fold in the top and bottom tips at the creases.

6 Using the creases you made in step 2, do an outside reverse fold.

8 Move the 2 corners to the sides. These will become the fins.

The side fins have been moved into position.

Hold onto the bases of the fins and pull to the left and right.

9 Press the structure inside the mouth to the side with your finger.

Once you have pressed it, pinch the whole side, including the side fin, to gather the layers there with a crease.

Finished

Stick on the eyes.

CHOMP

DOWN THE HATCH!

The Loch Ness Monster

A long-necked sea serpent that shows itself in the lake when the fog is dense. When it breaks the surface, the roiling water forms huge waves!

Attack Power	★ ★ ★ ★ ★
Defense Power	★ ★ ★
Magic Power	★ ★ ★ ★
Special Abilities	Produces a deadly whirlpool with its fins and long neck.

VIDEO
Type this URL into your browser:
tuttlepublishing.com/origami-monsters-and-magic

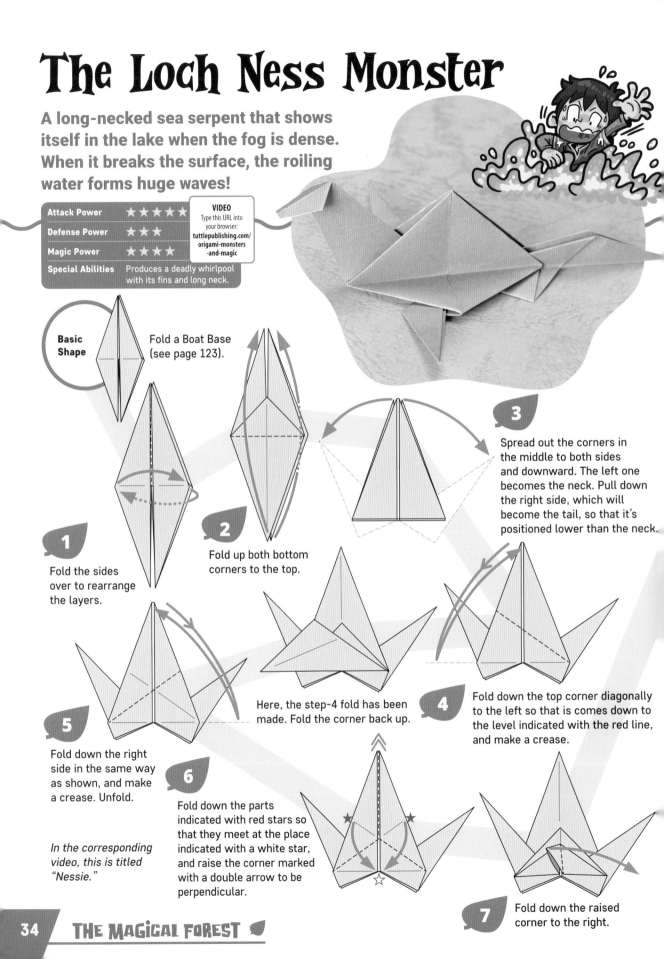

Basic Shape
Fold a Boat Base (see page 123).

1 Fold the sides over to rearrange the layers.

2 Fold up both bottom corners to the top.

3 Spread out the corners in the middle to both sides and downward. The left one becomes the neck. Pull down the right side, which will become the tail, so that it's positioned lower than the neck.

4 Fold down the top corner diagonally to the left so that is comes down to the level indicated with the red line, and make a crease.

5 Fold down the right side in the same way as shown, and make a crease. Unfold.

In the corresponding video, this is titled "Nessie."

Here, the step-4 fold has been made. Fold the corner back up.

6 Fold down the parts indicated with red stars so that they meet at the place indicated with a white star, and raise the corner marked with a double arrow to be perpendicular.

7 Fold down the raised corner to the right.

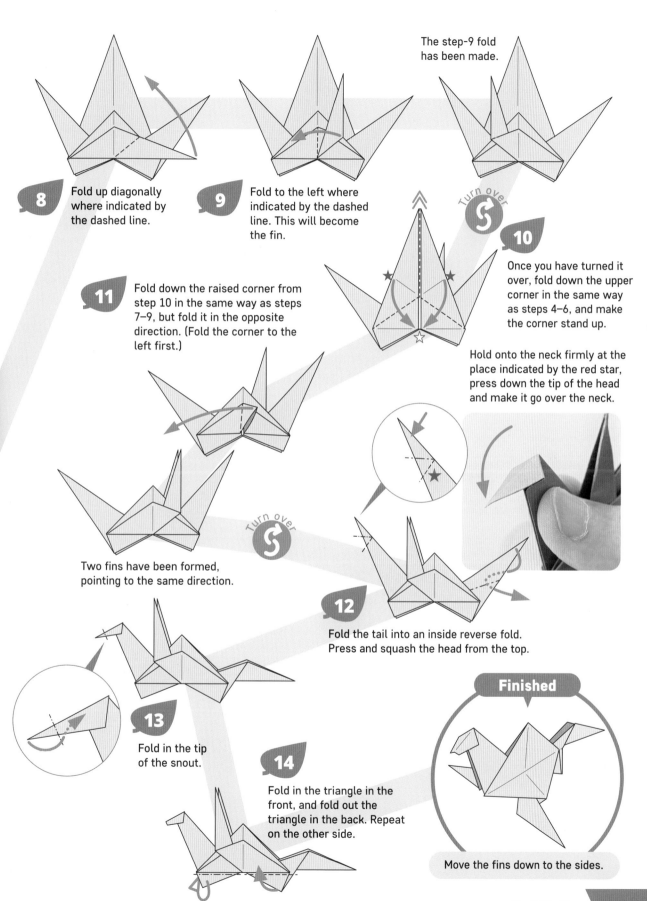

The step-9 fold has been made.

8 Fold up diagonally where indicated by the dashed line.

9 Fold to the left where indicated by the dashed line. This will become the fin.

Turn over

10 Once you have turned it over, fold down the upper corner in the same way as steps 4–6, and make the corner stand up.

Hold onto the neck firmly at the place indicated by the red star, press down the tip of the head and make it go over the neck.

11 Fold down the raised corner from step 10 in the same way as steps 7–9, but fold it in the opposite direction. (Fold the corner to the left first.)

Two fins have been formed, pointing to the same direction.

Turn over

12 Fold the tail into an inside reverse fold. Press and squash the head from the top.

13 Fold in the tip of the snout.

14 Fold in the triangle in the front, and fold out the triangle in the back. Repeat on the other side.

Finished

Move the fins down to the sides.

Magical Forest

The monsters are chasing us!

Escape into the School of Magic!

TRAINING AT THE SCHOOL OF MAGIC

We still can't defeat the monsters!
Let's study magic at this school and obtain
some enchanted items to help us bring the
creatures of the magic world to our side!

School of Magic

The Magician's Hat

This is part of the uniform at the School of Magic. By just wearing it, your magic powers increase!

Practicality	★	
Endurance	★ ★	**VIDEO** Type this URL into your browser: tuttlepublishing.com/ origami-monsters -and-magic
Magic Powers	★ ★ ★	
Characteristic	A pointed hat is the symbol of a magician.	

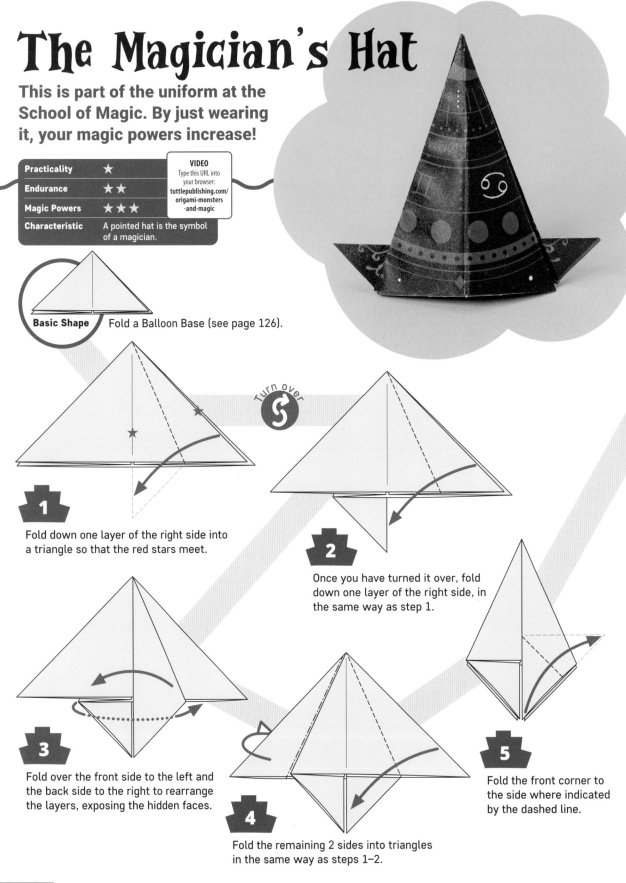

Basic Shape Fold a Balloon Base (see page 126).

Turn over

1 Fold down one layer of the right side into a triangle so that the red stars meet.

2 Once you have turned it over, fold down one layer of the right side, in the same way as step 1.

3 Fold over the front side to the left and the back side to the right to rearrange the layers, exposing the hidden faces.

4 Fold the remaining 2 sides into triangles in the same way as steps 1–2.

5 Fold the front corner to the side where indicated by the dashed line.

In the corresponding video, this is titled "Witch Hat."

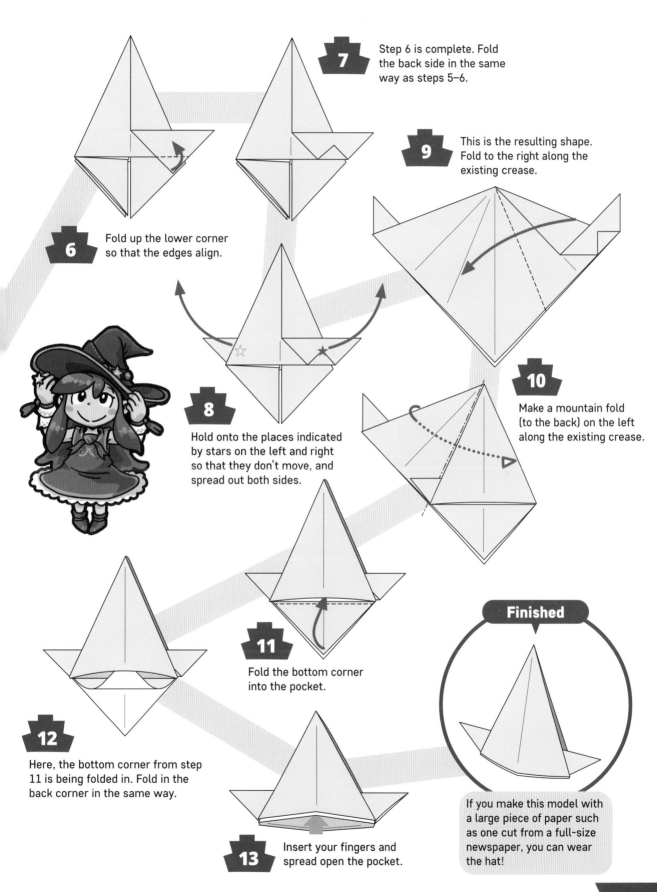

7 Step 6 is complete. Fold the back side in the same way as steps 5–6.

9 This is the resulting shape. Fold to the right along the existing crease.

6 Fold up the lower corner so that the edges align.

8 Hold onto the places indicated by stars on the left and right so that they don't move, and spread out both sides.

10 Make a mountain fold (to the back) on the left along the existing crease.

11 Fold the bottom corner into the pocket.

12 Here, the bottom corner from step 11 is being folded in. Fold in the back corner in the same way.

13 Insert your fingers and spread open the pocket.

Finished

If you make this model with a large piece of paper such as one cut from a full-size newspaper, you can wear the hat!

Magic Wand

Only those who have mastered magic can command a magic wand. If you make it with iridescent paper, its magic power may increase!

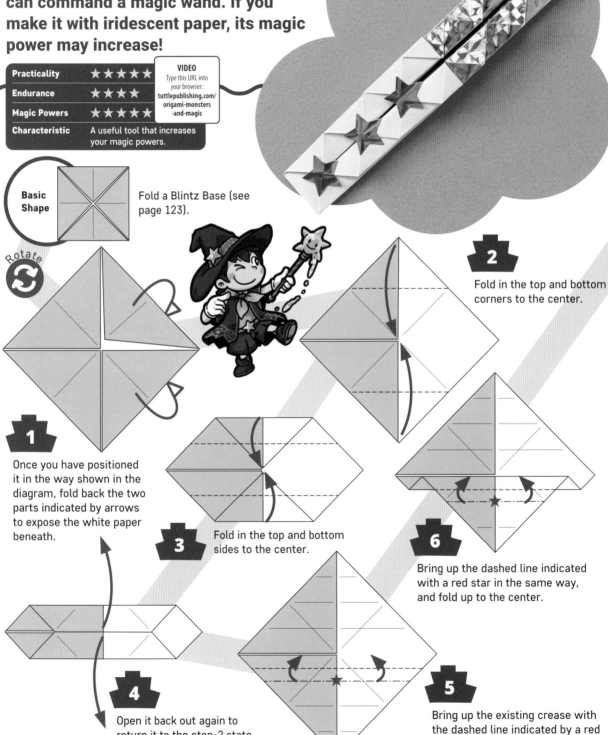

Practicality	★★★★★
Endurance	★★★★
Magic Powers	★★★★★
Characteristic	A useful tool that increases your magic powers.

VIDEO
Type this URL into your browser:
tuttlepublishing.com/origami-monsters-and-magic

Basic Shape — Fold a Blintz Base (see page 123).

Rotate

1 Once you have positioned it in the way shown in the diagram, fold back the two parts indicated by arrows to expose the white paper beneath.

2 Fold in the top and bottom corners to the center.

3 Fold in the top and bottom sides to the center.

4 Open it back out again to return it to the step-2 state.

5 Bring up the existing crease with the dashed line indicated by a red star into a mountain fold, and fold it up to the center.

6 Bring up the dashed line indicated with a red star in the same way, and fold up to the center.

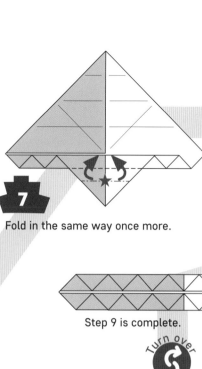

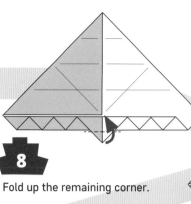

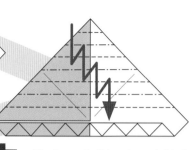

7 Fold in the same way once more.

8 Fold up the remaining corner.

9 The lower half has been folded into a zig-zag pattern. Fold down the upper part in the same way following steps 5–8.

Step 9 is complete.

Turn over

10 Once you have turned it over, insert your fingers where indicated by squat arrows and spread open the paper.

11 The right side corner will stand up, so fold it inward and flatten it.

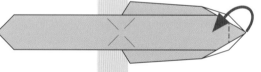

12 Fold in both sides again.

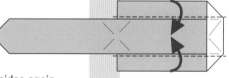

Step 12 is complete.

Turn over

Let the magic happen!

Presto! ♥

If you chant a spell, you'll feel like you can really make magic happen!

Finished

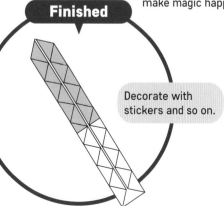

Decorate with stickers and so on.

Magic Lamp

When you rub this, a genie comes out and grants you three wishes. It's not suitable for making tea!

Practicality	★★★★★
Endurance	★★★
Magic Powers	★★★★★
Characteristic	A powerful genie lives inside.

VIDEO
Type this URL into your browser:
tuttlepublishing.com/origami-monsters-and-magic

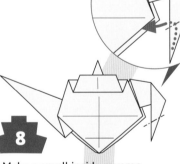

Basic Shape

Fold a Crane Base (see page 127).

Rotate

1

Once you have changed the direction from top to bottom, fold up both bottom corners.

2

Fold the bottom corner up at the dashed line to the red star, make a firm crease and fold back out again.

3

Fold down the top flap so that the corner meets the bottom corner. Repeat on the back side.

4

Fold up to where the position indicated by red dashed lines. Repeat on the back side.

5

Fold up to the red line. Repeat on the back side.

This side is the spout of the lamp

This side is the handle of the lamp

6

Pull the left corner to the side and shift it downward. Fold the right corner in an inside reverse fold.

8

Make a small inside reverse fold at the tip.

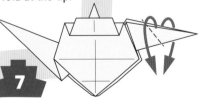

7

Fold the handle. Make a crease where indicated by the dashed line, and make an outside reverse fold.

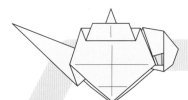

The step 7–8 folds have been completed. The handle is done.

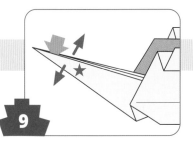

9

This is a close-up of the spout. Pinch the part marked with a red star firmly, insert a finger where indicated by the squat arrow and spread open.

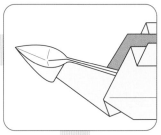

The spout has been spread open.

Rotate

When the bottom is square, pinch and smooth it out so it becomes flat.

Start with the blue arrows, and then pull the red arrows.

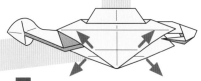

10

Rotate the base toward you and form the bottom. Pull diagonally and make the bottom square and flat.

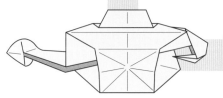

The bottom is formed.

Rotate

11

This is a close-up of the lid. Open up one layer of the front to expose the inside.

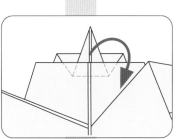

12

Pull out the hidden triangle.

Finished

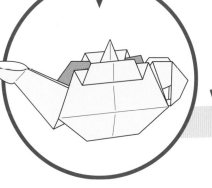

13

Pull out the hidden triangle on the front side too. After pulling out the triangles, close the lid.

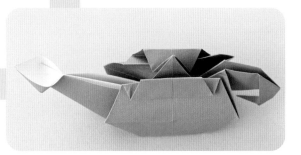

Riding Broom

Fly wherever you want with this magic item. But beware its sassy temperament toward amateur magic users.

Practicality	★★★★
Endurance	★★
Magic Powers	★★★
Characteristic	Allows you to fly high and fast.

VIDEO
Type this URL into your browser:
tuttlepublishing.com/origami-monsters-and-magic

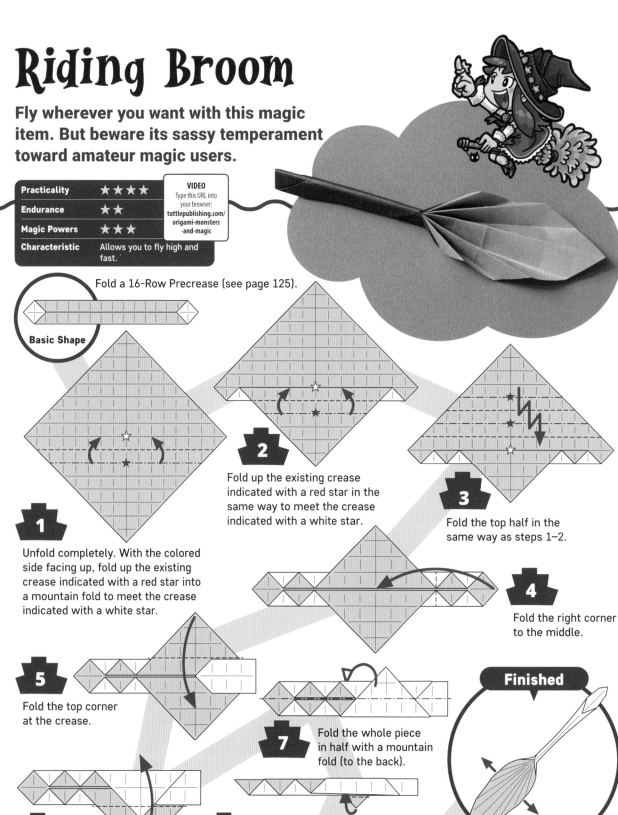

Fold a 16-Row Precrease (see page 125).

Basic Shape

1
Unfold completely. With the colored side facing up, fold up the existing crease indicated with a red star into a mountain fold to meet the crease indicated with a white star.

2
Fold up the existing crease indicated with a red star in the same way to meet the crease indicated with a white star.

3
Fold the top half in the same way as steps 1–2.

4
Fold the right corner to the middle.

5
Fold the top corner at the crease.

6
Fold up the bottom corner at the crease.

7
Fold the whole piece in half with a mountain fold (to the back).

8
Fold up the corner that is sticking out and insert it into the slot.

Step 8 is complete.

Rotate

Finished

Spread out to both sides to form a broom-like shape.

In the corresponding video, this is titled "Broomstick."

 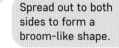

Messenger Owl

If you ask it to carry a message, it will go to deliver it at any cost. It is very loyal to the magician that owns it.

Practicality	★ ★ ★
Endurance	★ ★ ★
Magic Powers	★ ★
Characteristic	Delivers messages to others. Intelligent.

VIDEO
Type this URL into your browser:
tuttlepublishing.com/ origami-monsters -and-magic

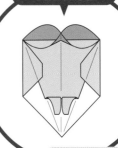

Basic Shape

Turn over

Fold a Crane Base (see page 127), and then fold the upper diamond shape back out into a square.

1

Make 2 creases using valley folds, and then fold in the parts where indicated by red stars and insert them into the sides.

Here, the lower corner is being opened up a bit and the right-side red-star part is being pushed in.

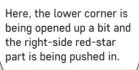

① ②

2

Fold the (1) corner at the dashed line, and then fold down again at the (2) line.

Return the corner down and flatten. Fold the left side in the same way.

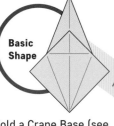

4

Fold the 2 lower corners upward, and fold down the top corner to stand perpendicular.

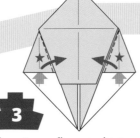

3

Insert your fingers where indicated by squat arrows, fold where indicated by red stars and flatten.

5

Curl the talons using a large straw or other similar item. Open up the upper pockets to form the eyes.

6

Fold back small portions of the corners with mountain folds to the inside.

In the corresponding video, this is titled "Owl on Finger."

Finished

Use the rounded talons to perch the owl on your finger!

Cat Familiar

A servant of the magician.
Because it is a cat, it will occasionally
pounce at you on a whim.

Practicality	★★★	
Endurance	★★	
Magic Powers	★★★	
Characteristic	It thinks it's your equal.	

VIDEO
Type this URL into
your browser:
tuttlepublishing.com/
origami-monsters
-and-magic

Basic Shape Fold an 8-Row
Precrease (1) (see
page 124).

Turn over

1 Once you have turned it over, fold
diagonally twice in the shaded squares as
shown to form X-shaped creases.

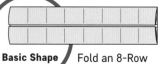

2 Make X-shaped creases in the adjacent 4
squares too.

3 Fold the 2 corners on the left into triangles
and fold out again to make creases.

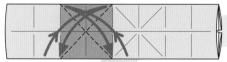

4 Open up the paper on the back to
the top and bottom by one row.

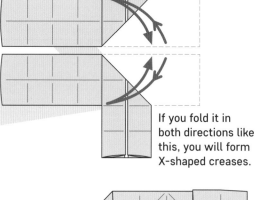

If you fold it in
both directions like
this, you will form
X-shaped creases.

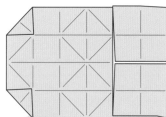

Step 5 is complete.

5 Fold the two left corners into
triangles. Fold in the 2 columns
on the right as shown.

*In the corresponding
video, this is titled
"Black Cat-in-the-Box."*

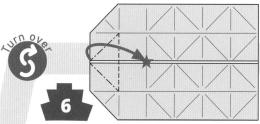

Turn over

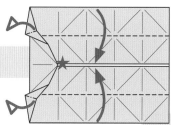

7

Fold in the top and bottom sides to the middle. The corners on the left that stand up will become the ears. Pull them out and make them pointy.

6

After you have turned the paper over top to bottom, fold the left side at the dashed lines so that a point is made that meets the red star mark.

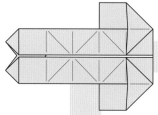

Here, the paper has been opened up and flattened at the top and bottom.

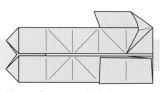

Here, the paper is being opened up to the top. Press it flat.

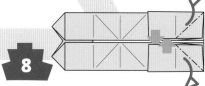

8

Insert your fingers at the places marked by squat arrows to spread out the middles, and flatten them out to the top and bottom.

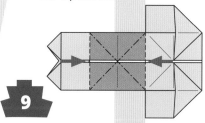

9

Press in the 4 shaded squares from the left and right, forming it into a three-dimensional X shape to make a spring.

MEOW!

The back of the piece. Press the X-shaped spring downward to hide the cat's head.

When you release your finger, the head will spring up!

Finished

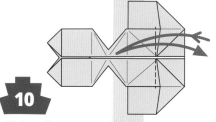

10

Make a firm crease where indicated by the dashed line.

The inside and the outside will separate, and the inside will become a spring, and the outside, a box.

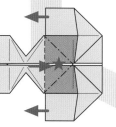

11

Make the 4 squares next to the step-9 region into a spring too. Press in the part marked with a red star to the right and make the X-shaped creases stand up as mountain folds.

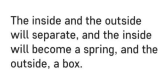

Rotate

Neaten up the body so it becomes a box shape, and apply the eyes and other facial features!

Mandrake

A mysterious plant whose roots are shaped like human limbs. If you try to pull it out of the ground, it screams!

Practicality	★ ★ ★	
Endurance	None	
Magic Powers	★ ★ ★	
Characteristic	It becomes an ingredient for painkillers and magic spells.	

VIDEO
Type this URL into your browser:
tuttlepublishing.com/ origami-monsters -and-magic

Basic Shape Fold an 8-Row Precrease (1) (see page 124).

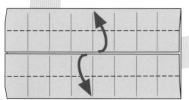

1 Open up one row each at the top and bottom so that it forms the shape shown. Fold inward to the middle.

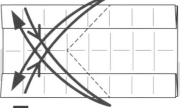

2 Make 2 diagonal folds to make creases.

Fold step 2 in this way. Make the creases only where marked with red stars.

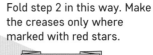

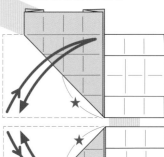

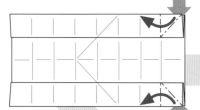

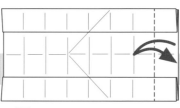

3 Refold the rightmost crease to make re-establish it as a valley crease.

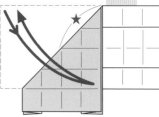

4 Insert your fingers where indicated by squat arrows, open up toward the crease and flatten.

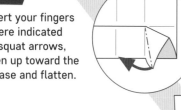

5 If you fold in diagonally where indicated by the red stars, the whole left side will stand up.

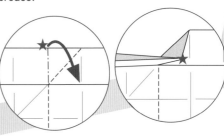

This is a close-up of the part marked with a red star. Press from the back with your fingers and fold into a triangle.

In the corresponding video, this is titled "Mandragora."

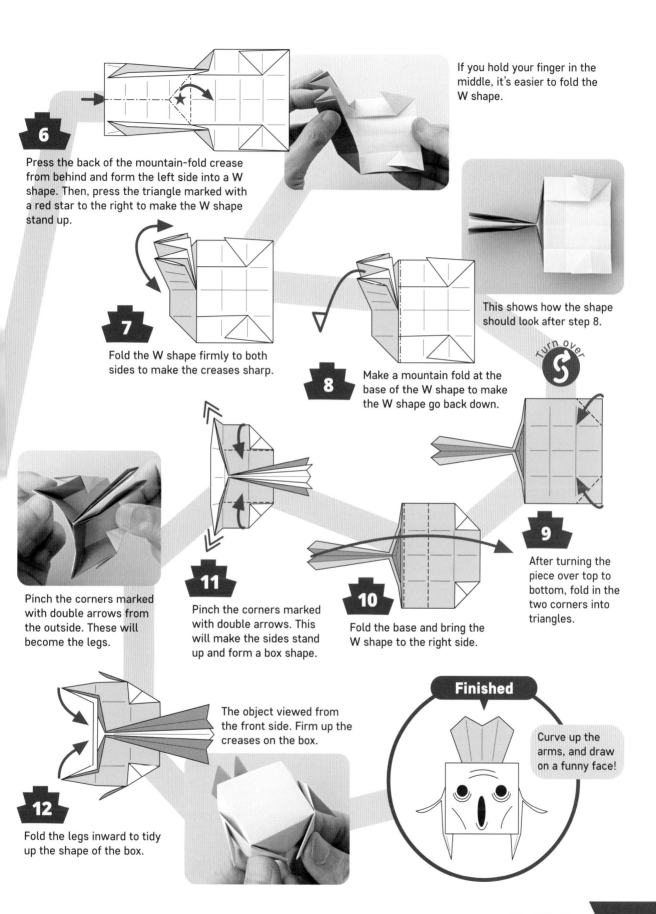

If you hold your finger in the middle, it's easier to fold the W shape.

6

Press the back of the mountain-fold crease from behind and form the left side into a W shape. Then, press the triangle marked with a red star to the right to make the W shape stand up.

This shows how the shape should look after step 8.

7

Fold the W shape firmly to both sides to make the creases sharp.

8

Make a mountain fold at the base of the W shape to make the W shape go back down.

Turn over

9

After turning the piece over top to bottom, fold in the two corners into triangles.

Pinch the corners marked with double arrows from the outside. These will become the legs.

11

Pinch the corners marked with double arrows. This will make the sides stand up and form a box shape.

10

Fold the base and bring the W shape to the right side.

The object viewed from the front side. Firm up the creases on the box.

Finished

Curve up the arms, and draw on a funny face!

12

Fold the legs inward to tidy up the shape of the box.

Unicorn

In contrast to its elegant equine appearance, the unicorn has an aggressive personality, and its horn isn't just for looks! If you manage to tame it, it becomes a strong ally.

Attack Power	★★★★	
Defense Power	★★★★	
Magic Power	★★★★★	
Special Abilities	The thrust of its horn and its powerful kick.	

VIDEO
Type this URL into your browser:
tuttlepublishing.com/origami-monsters-and-magic

Basic Shape Fold a 16-Row Precrease (see page 125).

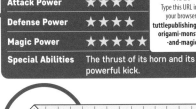

1 Unfold completely. Alternate between valley folds and mountain folds from the bottom and fold up to the center line, marked with a red star.

2 Fold down the top half in mirror image to step 1.

Center

3 This is a close-up of the right side. Insert your fingers where indicated by the squat arrows, fold diagonally and open up the inside.

4 Once the paper is standing up, fold to the left and press flat.

5 Insert your fingers where indicated by the squat arrows, and spread out in the direction of the long arrows.

A close-up of the middle being spread out. Flatten.

6 Fold the part that stands up to the right and flatten.

7 Insert your fingers where indicated by the squat arrows, spread out the middle and make diagonal folds as shown.

8 Fold the part that is standing up to the left and flatten.

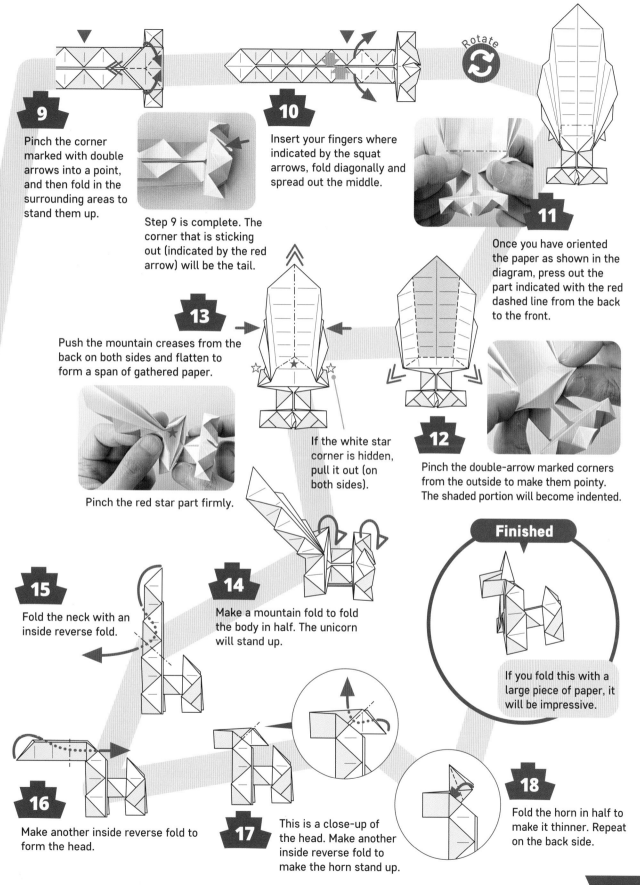

9

Pinch the corner marked with double arrows into a point, and then fold in the surrounding areas to stand them up.

Step 9 is complete. The corner that is sticking out (indicated by the red arrow) will be the tail.

10

Insert your fingers where indicated by the squat arrows, fold diagonally and spread out the middle.

Rotate

11

Once you have oriented the paper as shown in the diagram, press out the part indicated with the red dashed line from the back to the front.

13

Push the mountain creases from the back on both sides and flatten to form a span of gathered paper.

Pinch the red star part firmly.

If the white star corner is hidden, pull it out (on both sides).

12

Pinch the double-arrow marked corners from the outside to make them pointy. The shaded portion will become indented.

Finished

If you fold this with a large piece of paper, it will be impressive.

15

Fold the neck with an inside reverse fold.

14

Make a mountain fold to fold the body in half. The unicorn will stand up.

16

Make another inside reverse fold to form the head.

17

This is a close-up of the head. Make another inside reverse fold to make the horn stand up.

18

Fold the horn in half to make it thinner. Repeat on the back side.

Phoenix

A mythical magic bird that jumps into the flames when its life has ended, burning up and then being reborn. It is an incarnation of fire.

Attack Power	★★★★★	
Defense Power	★★★★	
Magic Power	★★★★★	
Special Abilities	The red hot flames that burst out from its wings and beak.	

VIDEO
Type this URL into your browser:
tuttlepublishing.com/origami-monsters-and-magic

Basic Shape Fold a 16-Row Precrease (see page 125).

1
Unfold completely. With the colored side facing up, make creases around the center 4 squares (shaded).

Step 1 is folded in this way. Fold horizontally and vertically and make creases only where marked by red stars.

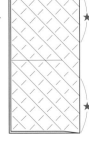

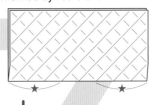

2
Indent the creases made in step 1 (the red lines) and the shaded parts. If you make mountain folds first, it will be easier to indent them.

3
The object will look a little like a starfish. Make folds at the valley creases (the red lines) to make the inside of the triangles pop back out. Do the same on all 4 sides.

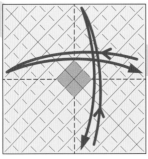

Step 5 is complete.

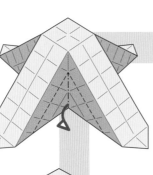

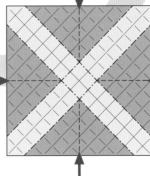

4
Make the inner triangles (marked by red mountain fold lines) pop back inside. Do the same on all 4 sides.

5
Firm up all creases and make the parts that stick out into columns.

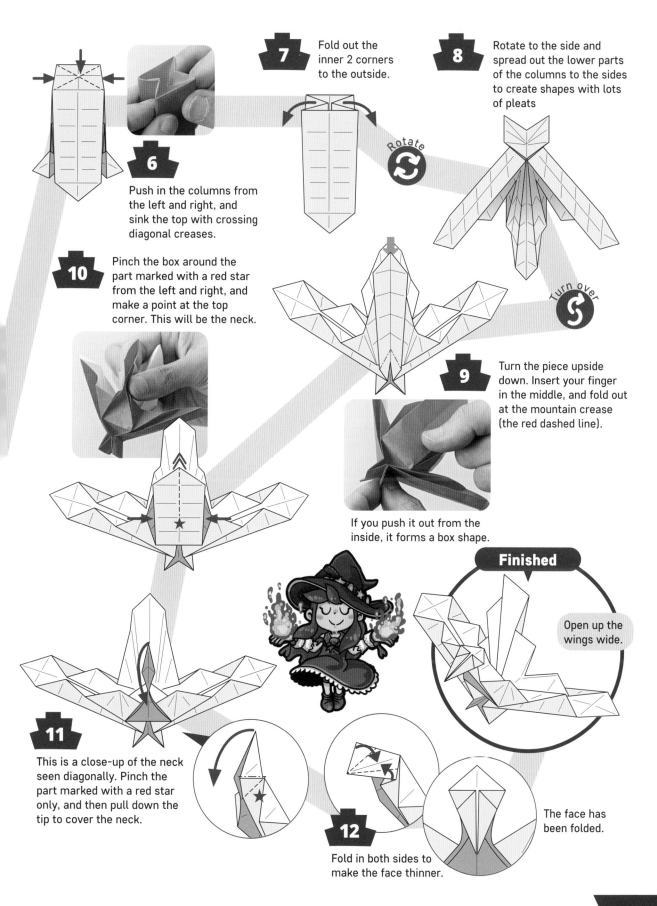

7 Fold out the inner 2 corners to the outside.

8 Rotate to the side and spread out the lower parts of the columns to the sides to create shapes with lots of pleats

6 Push in the columns from the left and right, and sink the top with crossing diagonal creases.

Rotate

Turn over

10 Pinch the box around the part marked with a red star from the left and right, and make a point at the top corner. This will be the neck.

9 Turn the piece upside down. Insert your finger in the middle, and fold out at the mountain crease (the red dashed line).

If you push it out from the inside, it forms a box shape.

Finished

Open up the wings wide.

11 This is a close-up of the neck seen diagonally. Pinch the part marked with a red star only, and then pull down the tip to cover the neck.

12 Fold in both sides to make the face thinner.

The face has been folded.

Magic "House-Key"

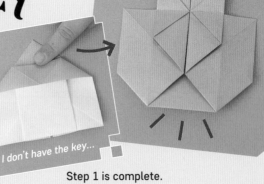

I found it!

I don't have the key...

It's the start of qualification exams to see if you've become a full-fledged magician! The first test is a spell that transforms a house into a key.

Magic Difficulty	★
Entertainment Value	★★★
Tip	When transforming the house into a key, slide your finger in the right way.

VIDEO
Type this URL into your browser:
tuttlepublishing.com/
origami-monsters
-and-magic

Basic Shape

Rotate

Fold a Blintz Base (see page 123).

1

Fold the top and bottom corners to the middle.

Step 1 is complete.

Turn over

2

Once you have turned the piece over, fold it in half, and then unfold it to form a crease.

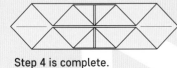

Step 4 is complete.

4

Fold in the top and bottom corners to the center.

3

Fold the top and bottom sides to the center. Do not fold the paper on the back side—let it swing out to the front.

Turn over

5

Once you have turned it over, insert your fingers where indicated by the squat arrows and spread out.

Turn over **Rotate**

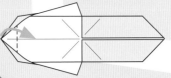

6

The left side corner will stand up, so fold it to the inside and flatten.

Step 6 is complete.

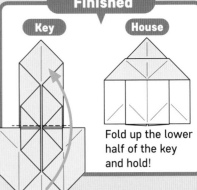

Fold up the lower half of the key and hold!

In the corresponding video, this is titled "House Changes Key."

Haunted Chair

The second test is a chair that stands up on its own. If you release the finger that is holding it down, it will twist and spring up to become a chair!

Spring!

Magic Difficulty	★ ★
Entertainment Value	★ ★ ★ ★
Tip	Hold down the chair lightly with just the tip of your finger, and release it as if you were stroking the chair.

VIDEO
Type this URL into your browser:
tuttlepublishing.com/origami-monsters-and-magic

Basic Shape

Fold an 8-Row Precrease (1) (see page 124).

1 Make a fold to the 2nd line from the left from the left and right edges at the dashed lines along existing creases.

2 Fold in the right side corners narrowly starting from points around ⅓ of the distance to the horizontal center line.

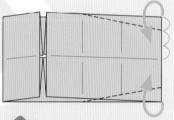

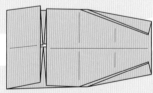

Step 2 is complete.

Turn over

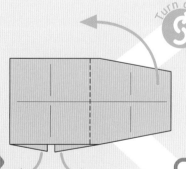

3 Once you have turned it over, fold up the right side to form the back of the chair. Stand up the legs of the chair on the back side too.

Finished

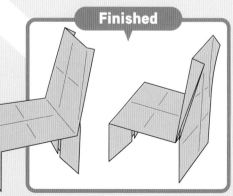

Collapse the chair with the back facing down. Press your finger on the part marked with a red star, and then release it to trigger the spring.

In the corresponding video, this is titled "Magical Rising Chair."

School of Magic Graduation Test (3)

Magic Soft Serve Ice Cream Cone

The last test is a soft serve ice cream that disappears. You want to bite into it, and then...what? It's gone!

It disappeared!?

Magic Difficulty	★ ★ ★
Entertainment Value	★ ★ ★ ★ ★
Tip	This magic is a big hit when it succeeds. If you can polish your acting skills too, even better.

VIDEO
Type this URL into your browser:
tuttlepublishing.com/
origami-monsters
-and-magic

1
Fold the paper in half corner to corner both ways and unfold to make 2 creases.

Turn over

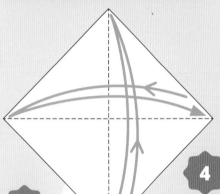

2
Once you have turned the paper over, fold the top edges to the center line as shown.

Step 2 is complete.

Crease only along the length marked by the red star. Unfold.

4
Fold the double-circle edges together, and make a crease where indicated by the dashed line.

Turn over

3
Once you have turned it over, fold in the lower edges to the center line.

5
Make a crease in the same way on the right side by folding the double-circle marked edges together.

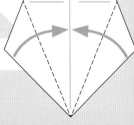

In the corresponding video, this is titled "Magical Ice Cream."

6 Open up the lower part.

Step 7 is complete.

Turn over ↻

7 Once you have turned it over, place the edges marked with double circles together and fold to form triangular flaps.

Turn over ↻

Fold only along the length marked by the red star.

Step 10 is complete.

10 Place the edges marked with double circles together and fold to make 2 creases indicated by the dashed lines. This is the same fold as steps 4–5.

9 Fold in the left and right bottom edges at the creases.

8 Once you have turned it over, fold in the corners that are sticking out.

Your acting skills are important for magic too!

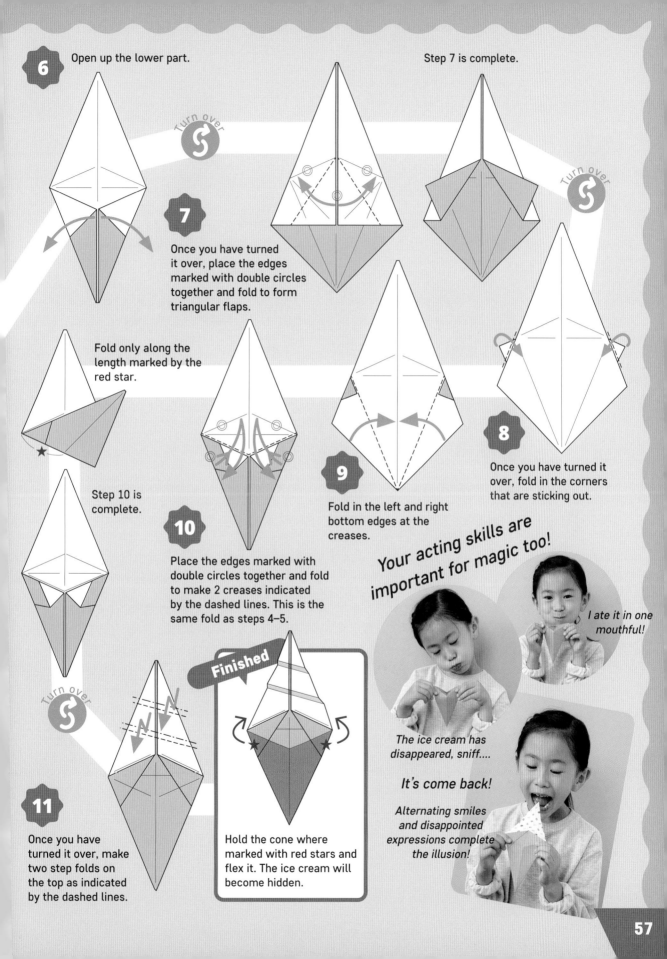

I ate it in one mouthful!

Turn over ↻

11 Once you have turned it over, make two step folds on the top as indicated by the dashed lines.

Finished

Hold the cone where marked with red stars and flex it. The ice cream will become hidden.

The ice cream has disappeared, sniff....

It's come back!

Alternating smiles and disappointed expressions complete the illusion!

57

We've graduated from the School of Magic!

School of Magic

Next, we'll obtain weapons to power up!

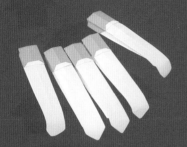

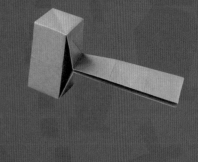

GETTING EQUIPPED IN THE WEAPON SHOP

The weapon shop in town has a lot of weapons that are necessary for fighting monsters. Can we get our hands on swords, shields, throwing stars, war hammers and so on?

Flexible Sword

A weapon that is indispensable to adventures, as well as the being the first step to becoming a hero. Even when it clashes with another weapon, the blade does not chip.

Attack Power	★ ★ ★ ★
Defense Power	★ ★ ★
Price	★ ★ ★ ★
Characteristics	Flexible with a sharp blade.

VIDEO
Type this URL into your browser:
tuttlepublishing.com/origami-monsters-and-magic

Basic Shape Fold an 8-Row Precrease (1) (see page 124).

5 Continue to fold valley folds and mountain folds into the left half of the paper in the same way as step 3.

Fold the valley folds and mountain folds in steps while you pinch and squeeze the double-arrow-marked corner to make it pointed.

4 Indent the valley folds, and make the mountain folds stick out. This step will be easier if you pre-fold along the creases.

1 Unfold completely. Fold the paper in half corner to corner both ways and unfold to make 2 creases.

2 Fold in the top and bottom 1 square from the center as shown, to the points marked with red stars.

3 Pinch the corner marked with a double arrow into a mountain fold, as you make a mountain fold on the right-side rows marked with dashed lines.

In the corresponding video, this is titled "Flexible Katana Sword Long Version." You can see a video of a shorter "Flexible sword" on the SasaTube YouTube channel too (https://www.youtube.com/c/IsamuSasagawa).

6 Continue folding in the same way.

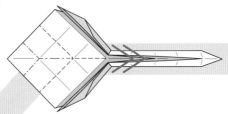

The paper after step 6 has been completed. Viewed from the diagonal.

8 Once you have placed the colored side on top, press the white-star part against the wall of the red-star part, and press in from the outside too.

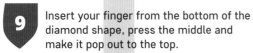

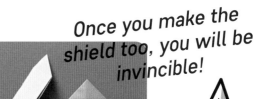

Turn over

7 After you have collapsed the paper, fold at the dashed lines to both sides to make firm creases.

If you hold and press at two places, a diamond shape will be formed.

Once you make the shield too, you will be invincible!

9 Insert your finger from the bottom of the diamond shape, press the middle and make it pop out to the top.

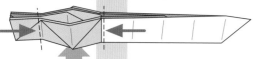

The Invincible Shield is on page 72.

Press the crease from the back.

Turn over   Rotate

10 If you fold the "hilt" up and down, the sword will become more flexible.

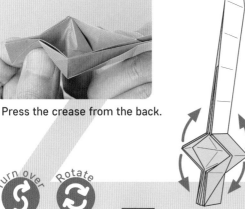

Finished

SPRRRING!

It bends so far!

Bolt Thrower

A weapon that launches cylindrical projectiles long distances to damage enemies that are far away.

Attack Power	★★★	
Defense Power	★	
Price	★★★	
Characteristics	It flexes like a spring to shoot missiles.	

VIDEO
Type this URL into your browser:
tuttlepublishing.com/origami-monsters-and-magic

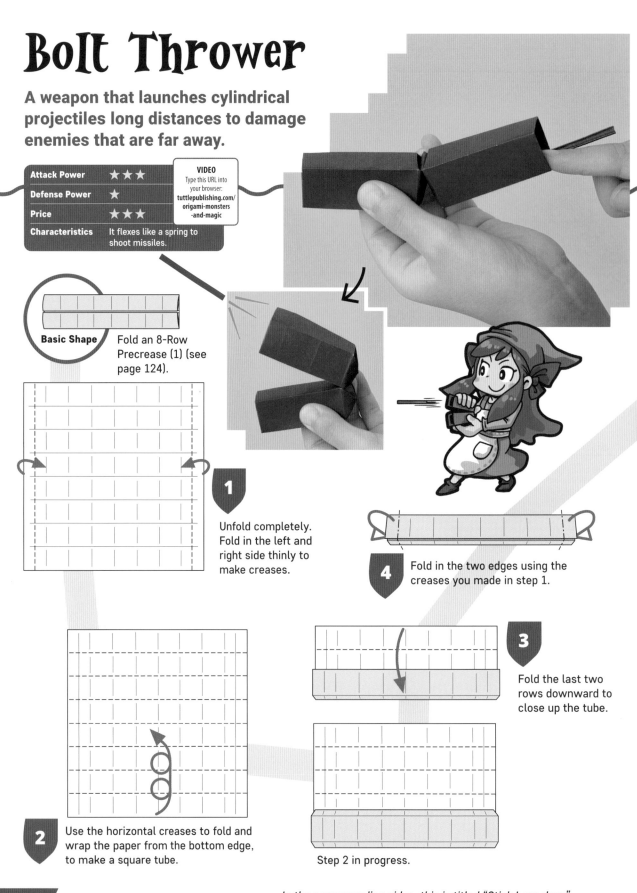

Basic Shape Fold an 8-Row Precrease (1) (see page 124).

1 Unfold completely. Fold in the left and right side thinly to make creases.

4 Fold in the two edges using the creases you made in step 1.

3 Fold the last two rows downward to close up the tube.

2 Use the horizontal creases to fold and wrap the paper from the bottom edge, to make a square tube.

Step 2 in progress.

In the corresponding video, this is titled "Stick Launcher."

The tube has been folded in.
Fold in the other side in the same way.

5 Press in the middle firmly.

The paper will
become indented
and bulge out.

6 Flatten the indented part carefully.

A close-up of the right side.
The edge is being pushed in.

Be careful not to over flatten
the tube. Insert your finger
into the tube as you flatten it.

Once the part has been
flattened, you can bend it.

7 The object seen from
the side. Bend the
tube down.

How to Make a Bolt Projectile
Cut a piece of origami paper into quarters,
or use small origami sheets that are about
3 inches (7.5 cm) square. Fold in half 4
times to make a thin projectile.

8 Fold in the parts that stick out.

Finished

Rotate

9 Fold in the connecting
parts of the tube to close
them up.

Bend down the tube
and release your finger.
The projectile will fly
when the tube flexes to
stand back up.

You only need to bend it lightly.
If you bend it too hard, the
spring function will weaken.

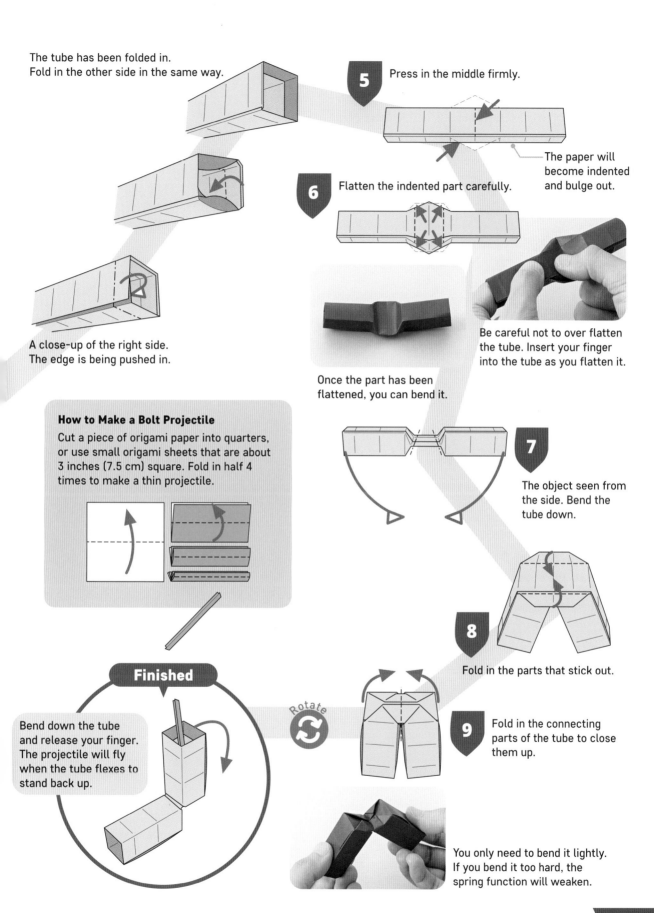

Self-Destruct Button

One never knows what will happen with these risky devices. Is it armed to explode?
Would you dare to press one?

Attack Power	?????
Defense Power	?????
Price	★
Characteristics	They're reputed to have great destructive power.

VIDEO
Type this URL into your browser:
tuttlepublishing.com/
origami-monsters
-and-magic

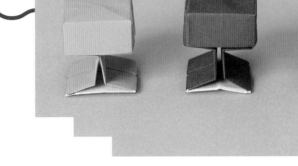

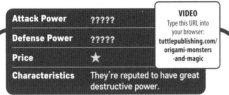

Basic Shape Fold an 8-Row Precrease (1) (see page 124).

1 Fold out one row on the top and bottom.

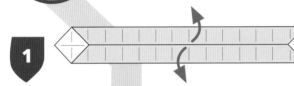

2 Fold so that the double circles and the red circles meet, and make 4 short creases.

The corners have become box-shaped.

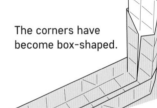

4 Fold over both sides of the part that stands up with mountain folds to the back.

Step 2 is folded in this way. Make creases only where marked by red stars.

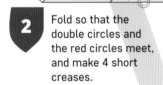

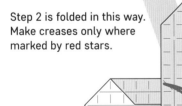

3 Pinch the red star creases and fold in the areas around the middle (the shaded part) and the right side will stand up.

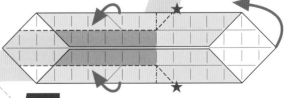

*In the corresponding video, this is titled "Dangerous Button 5."
You can watch videos for more origami buttons on the "SasaTube"
YouTube channel (https://www.youtube.com/c/IsamuSasagawa).*

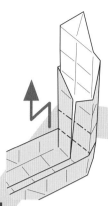

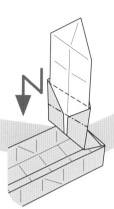

7 Fold back the tip.

The right-side folding sequence is complete.

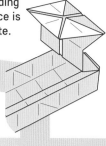

5 A close-up of the part that is standing up. Fold into a zig-zag shape with a valley fold and a mountain fold.

6 Next, fold into a zig-zag shape again with a mountain fold and a valley fold.

8 Fold the left side in the same way. If you pinch the creases marked with red stars, the left side will stand up.

It looks like this when viewed diagonally from the side.

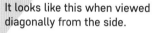

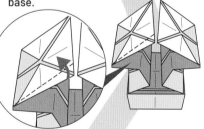

9 Once you have folded back both sides with mountain folds as in step 4, proceed in the same way as steps 5–7.

10 Fold in the edge of one side to make it narrower. This will become the base.

If you press it, what will happen?!

Who made this button, and for what purpose? According to the weapons merchant, "a heart-pounding experience is guaranteed!"

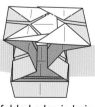

Finished

Turn over

11 Insert the narrowly folded edge from step 10 inside as shown.

The folded edge is being inserted. Seat it firmly.

The base has been assembled.

War Hammer

A blunt-force weapon that lets you destroy things when you pound it down. It's simple, but has great destructive power.

Attack Power	★ ★ ★ ★ ★
Defense Power	★
Price	★ ★
Characteristics	Increases the power of the holder.

VIDEO
Type this URL into your browser:
tuttlepublishing.com/origami-monsters-and-magic

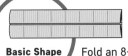

Basic Shape Fold an 8-Row Precrease (1) (see page 124).

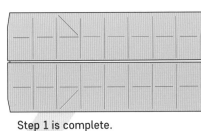

Step 1 is complete.

1 Fold out 1 row on the top and bottom to form the shape shown. Fold the points on the edges marked with double circles to meet the red circle to make 2 short creases.

Step 1 is folded in this way. Make creases only where marked with red stars, and then unfold.

Turn over

2 Once you have turned it over top to bottom, fold the points on the edges marked with double circles to meet the red circle to make 2 short creases.

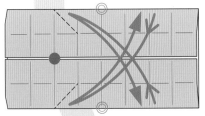

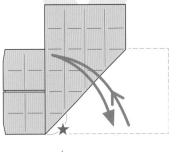

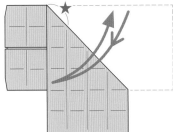

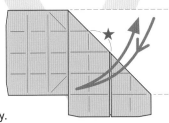

Step 2 is folded in this way. Make creases only where marked with red stars, and then unfold.

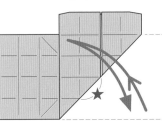

In the corresponding video, this is titled "Origami Hammer New Version."

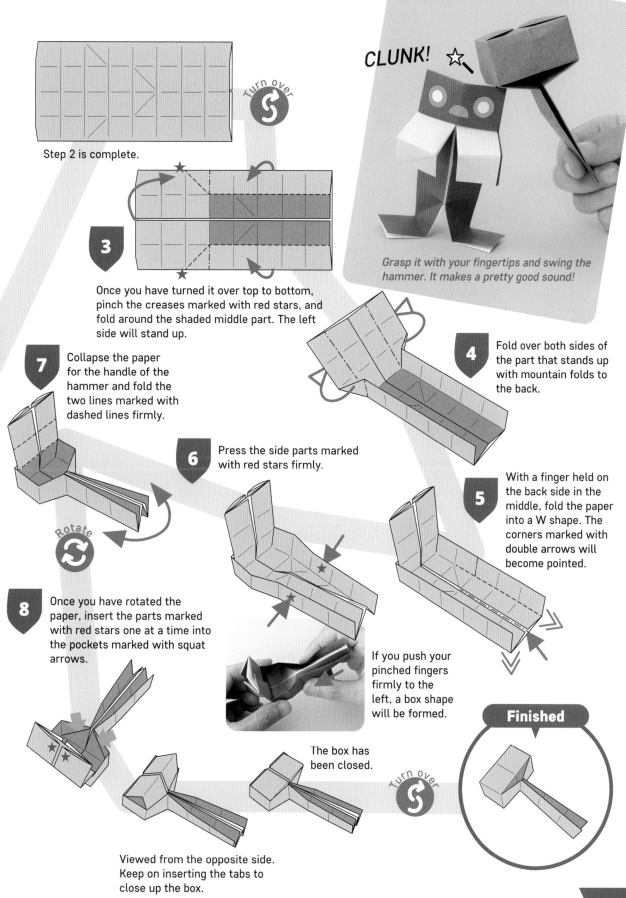

Step 2 is complete.

3 Once you have turned it over top to bottom, pinch the creases marked with red stars, and fold around the shaded middle part. The left side will stand up.

CLUNK! ☆

Grasp it with your fingertips and swing the hammer. It makes a pretty good sound!

4 Fold over both sides of the part that stands up with mountain folds to the back.

5 With a finger held on the back side in the middle, fold the paper into a W shape. The corners marked with double arrows will become pointed.

6 Press the side parts marked with red stars firmly.

If you push your pinched fingers firmly to the left, a box shape will be formed.

7 Collapse the paper for the handle of the hammer and fold the two lines marked with dashed lines firmly.

Rotate

8 Once you have rotated the paper, insert the parts marked with red stars one at a time into the pockets marked with squat arrows.

The box has been closed.

Turn over

Finished

Viewed from the opposite side. Keep on inserting the tabs to close up the box.

Ninja Star

This weapon is flicked to make it fly. This type is easier to aim than the type that is thrown, so it's popular with heroes.

Attack Power	★★★★	
Defense Power	None	
Price	★★★	
Characteristics	Increases the power of the holder.	

VIDEO
Type this URL into your browser:
tuttlepublishing.com/origami-monsters-and-magic

Basic Shape

Fold a Balloon Base (see page 126).

1 Fold the entire shape in half, and then unfold to make a crease. Make the crease very firmly.

2 Fold the top and bottom to the crease made in step 1 to make 2 more creases.

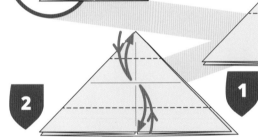

Collapse the corners by gradually pinching the creases,

3 All 3 creases have been made. Unfold completely.

4 Once you unfold the paper, you will see a lot of creases. Pinch the corners marked with double arrows into mountain folds and make them pointy, and fold the 1st rows of creases into mountain folds.

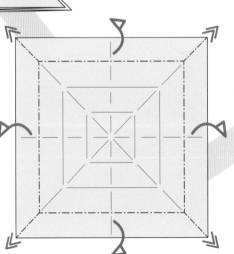

5 Push in from the outside all around, and make the valley folds indented and the mountain folds stick up.

In the corresponding video, this is titled "Finger Ninja Star."

Step 5 is complete. 4 narrow points have been formed.

6 Once you have turned it over, collapse in the walls of the middle box inward. The points will stand up.

7 Lay down all 4 points in the same direction (counterclockwise).

Turn over

It has formed a pinwheel shape.

8 Once you have turned it over, fold the right side point inward.

Turn over

9 Fold the upper point inward.

10 Fold the left point inward.

11 Lift up the part marked with a red star to form a gap, and then fold up the lower point and insert it into the gap.

12 Tug on the points to tidy up the shape.

Finished

Aim at your target, and flick the Throwing Star with your finger. It will fly quite a distance, so don't aim it toward anyone!

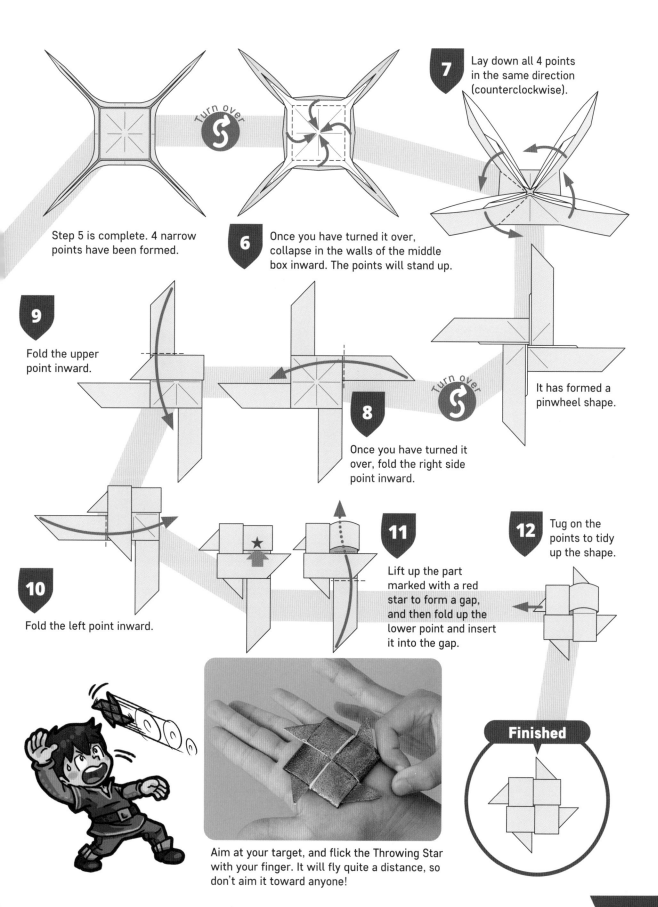

Battle Claws

A weapon for close combat situations. If you scratch your opponent with these pointed nails, you can score a critical hit.

Attack Power	★★★★★	
Defense Power	★★★	
Price	★★★★★	
Characteristics	Intimidating just by being worn.	

VIDEO
Type this URL into your browser:
tuttlepublishing.com/
origami-monsters
-and-magic

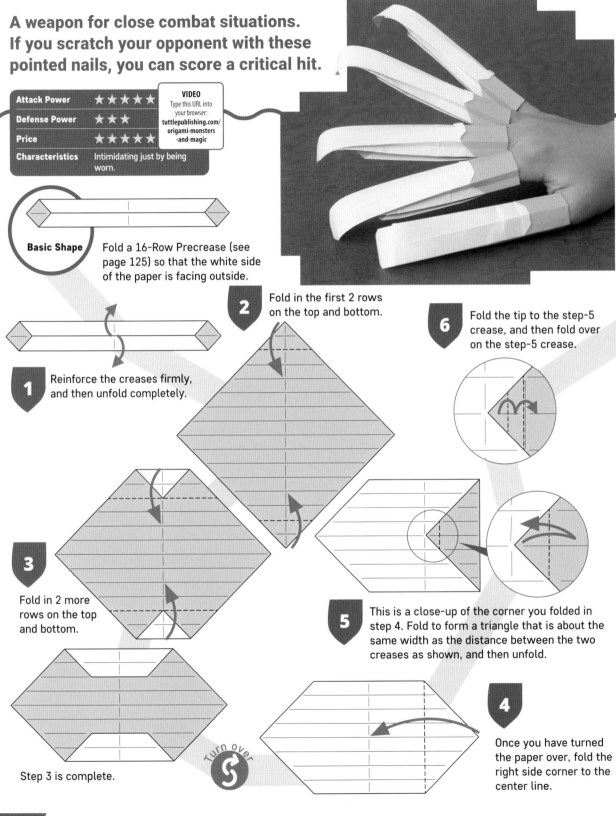

Basic Shape Fold a 16-Row Precrease (see page 125) so that the white side of the paper is facing outside.

1 Reinforce the creases firmly, and then unfold completely.

2 Fold in the first 2 rows on the top and bottom.

3 Fold in 2 more rows on the top and bottom.

Step 3 is complete.

Turn over

4 Once you have turned the paper over, fold the right side corner to the center line.

5 This is a close-up of the corner you folded in step 4. Fold to form a triangle that is about the same width as the distance between the two creases as shown, and then unfold.

6 Fold the tip to the step-5 crease, and then fold over on the step-5 crease.

In the corresponding video, this is titled "Loooong Nails."

8 Fold up 2 rows on the bottom, and insert the corner into the upper pocket.

Turn over

7 Once you have turned it over, fold down the top 3 rows.

9 Insert your fingers where indicated by the squat arrows, and form the whole piece into a rectangular tube.

Step 6 is complete.

10 Press your fingers on the sides, and indent between the corners of the tube.

The sides will become indented and look like this.

When you curl it, it looks more like a fingernail.

11 Curl the pointy end using a pencil or similar tool.

Turn over

Finished

Fold 5 or 10 of these and put them on your fingers!

The one on the right is made with a 6-inch (15-cm) square of origami paper, and the one on the left is made with a 4-inch (10-cm) paper. One made with 6-inch paper may be too large for a child's hands.

Looks fierce!

This is a photo of Battle Claws made with 4-inch square paper on a second grader's hand.

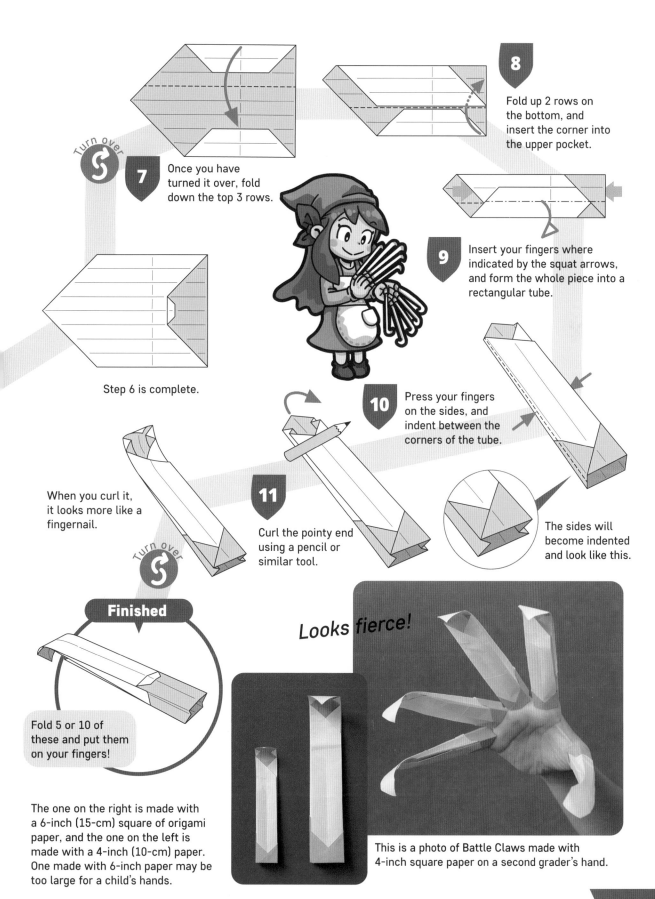

Invincible Shield

A shield that neutralizes enemy attacks. It's an item that is very useful when fighting an opponent who has stronger attack powers than you.

Attack Power	None
Defense Power	★★★★★
Price	★★★
Characteristics	Protects the bearer simply by being held.

VIDEO
Type this URL into your browser:
tuttlepublishing.com/ origami-monsters -and-magic

Basic Shape
Fold an 8-Row Precrease (1) (see page 124).

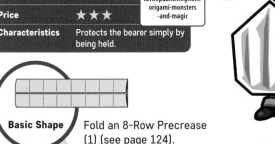

1 Open up the top and bottom rows to form this shape. Fold in the left corners as shown.

2 Fold the points on the edges marked with double circles to meet the red circle to form 2 diagonal creases.

Step 2 in progress. Make creases only through 2 rows, like those marked with the red star for the bottom fold illustrated below.

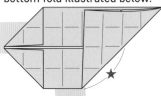

3 Fold over the 3 right columns.

4 Insert your fingers where indicated by the squat arrows, open up the top and bottom edges and flatten.

This shows the lower half being folded. Flatten as shown.

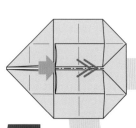

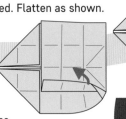

5 Lift up the part that was folded in step 4, and make a mountain fold in the center.

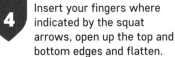

Rotate

Turn over

Finished

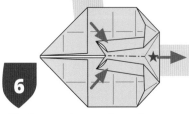

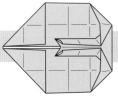

6 Pinch up and press down the center, and press toward the triangle marked by a red star on the right.

A handle has been formed, and the shield has become three-dimensional.

In the corresponding video, this is titled "Hero's Shield."

Cemetery

4

MIDNIGHT DUEL IN THE CEMETERY

Have you become stronger by obtaining magic powers and weapons? Test your mettle by fighting the monsters in the graveyard!

Lantern Ghost

This lantern lures people into the dark graveyard with its light, but then glares at them with its single baleful eye, immobilizing them. Be careful of the protruding tongue!

Attack Power	★ ★
Defense Power	★
Mystical Power	★ ★ ★
Special Abilities	Attacks by glaring at you and licking you.

VIDEO
Type this URL into your browser:
tuttlepublishing.com/
origami-monsters
-and-magic

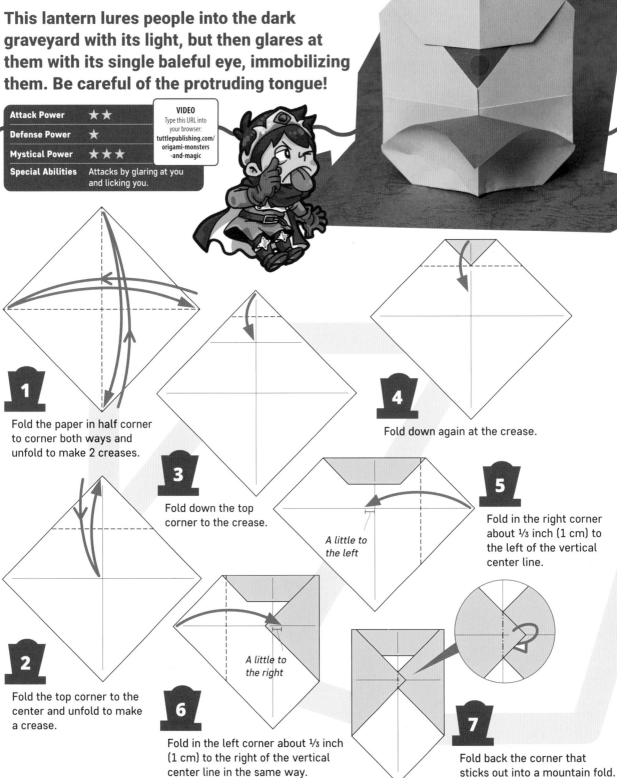

1 Fold the paper in half corner to corner both ways and unfold to make 2 creases.

2 Fold the top corner to the center and unfold to make a crease.

3 Fold down the top corner to the crease.

4 Fold down again at the crease.

5 Fold in the right corner about ⅓ inch (1 cm) to the left of the vertical center line.

A little to the left

A little to the right

6 Fold in the left corner about ⅓ inch (1 cm) to the right of the vertical center line in the same way.

7 Fold back the corner that sticks out into a mountain fold.

In the corresponding video, this is titled "Japanese Lantern Monster."

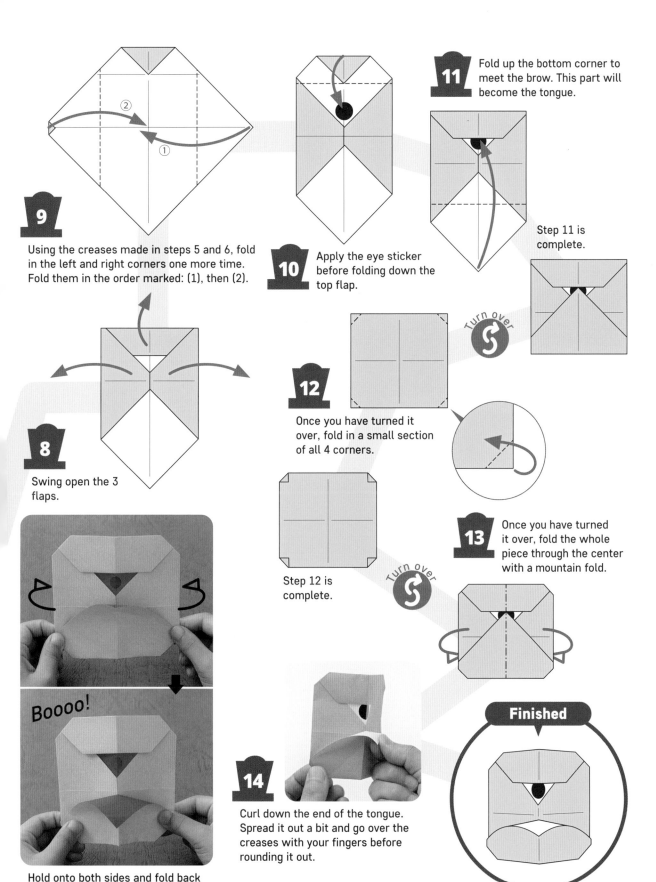

9

Using the creases made in steps 5 and 6, fold in the left and right corners one more time. Fold them in the order marked: (1), then (2).

8

Swing open the 3 flaps.

10

Apply the eye sticker before folding down the top flap.

11

Fold up the bottom corner to meet the brow. This part will become the tongue.

Step 11 is complete.

Turn over

12

Once you have turned it over, fold in a small section of all 4 corners.

Step 12 is complete.

Turn over

13

Once you have turned it over, fold the whole piece through the center with a mountain fold.

14

Curl down the end of the tongue. Spread it out a bit and go over the creases with your fingers before rounding it out.

Boooo!

Hold onto both sides and fold back slightly to make the tongue stick out.

Finished

Noodle-Necked Monster

This pale-faced fiend will doggedly chase you through the darkness. You must defeat it before it can wrap you with its long neck.

Attack Power	★ ★ ★
Defense Power	★ ★ ★
Mystical Power	★ ★ ★ ★
Special Abilities	Attacks you with its long extending neck.

VIDEO
Type this URL into your browser:
tuttlepublishing.com/
origami-monsters
-and-magic

Basic Shape — Fold a 16-Row Precrease (see page 125).

Turn over

1 Make creases as marked by red lines in the 3rd full squares from the left.

Step 1 is folded in this way. Make short creases only where marked by red stars, and then unfold.

Step 2 is folded in this way. Make short creases only where marked by red stars, and then unfold.

2 Make creases as marked by red lines in the 5th full squares from the right.

3 ① Press in both sides to indent the middle, and then ②–③ press firmly from the sides to make triangular walls where marked by red stars.

Step 3 is complete. Next, we will work with only the left side.

This is the part marked with a red star in the diagram.

The left side is being firmly pressed in.

In the corresponding video, this is titled "Long Neck Monster."

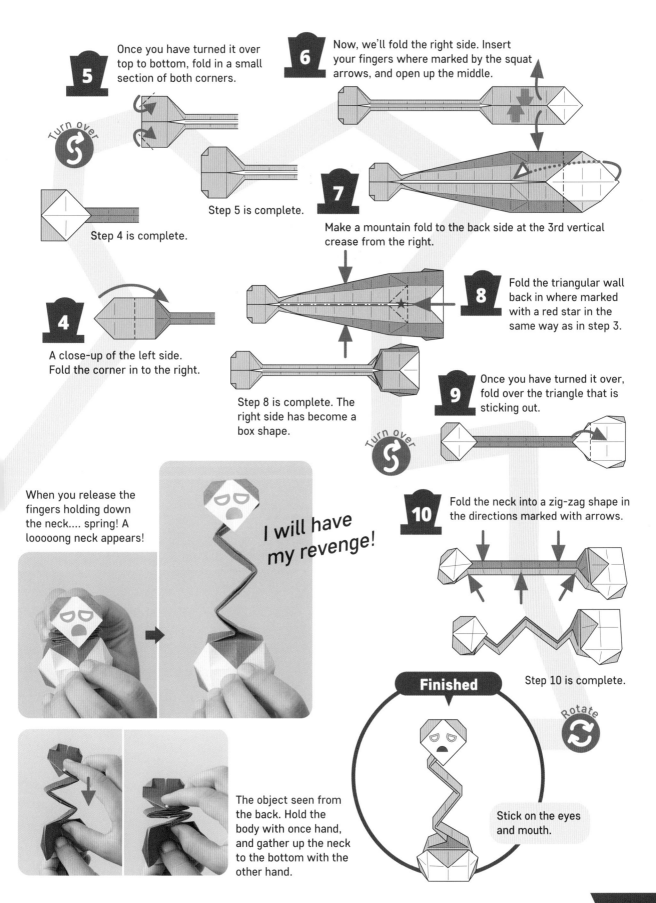

5 Once you have turned it over top to bottom, fold in a small section of both corners.

Turn over

Step 5 is complete.

Step 4 is complete.

4 A close-up of the left side. Fold the corner in to the right.

6 Now, we'll fold the right side. Insert your fingers where marked by the squat arrows, and open up the middle.

7 Make a mountain fold to the back side at the 3rd vertical crease from the right.

8 Fold the triangular wall back in where marked with a red star in the same way as in step 3.

Step 8 is complete. The right side has become a box shape.

9 Once you have turned it over, fold over the triangle that is sticking out.

Turn over

10 Fold the neck into a zig-zag shape in the directions marked with arrows.

Step 10 is complete.

When you release the fingers holding down the neck.... spring! A looooong neck appears!

I will have my revenge!

The object seen from the back. Hold the body with once hand, and gather up the neck to the bottom with the other hand.

Finished

Rotate

Stick on the eyes and mouth.

The "Disappearing" Ghost

This ghost frightens travelers by pretending it's not there. It's said it can be discouraged if you shout "There you are!" at it.

Attack Power	★	
Defense Power	★ ★	
Mystical Power	★	
Special Abilities	Pretends not to be there. A little slow-witted.	

VIDEO
Type this URL into your browser:
tuttlepublishing.com/origami-monsters-and-magic

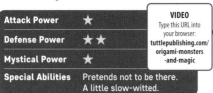

1

Place the origami paper with the colored side facing up. Fold the paper in half corner to corner both ways and unfold to make 2 creases.

2

Fold the top and bottom corners to the center.

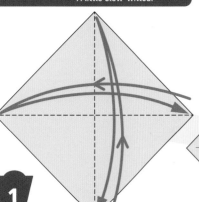

3

Fold the edges marked with red circles to the corresponding creases marked with double circles to make two diagonal creases as shown.

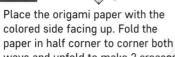

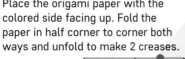

Step 3 is folded in this way. Be sure to make creases only where marked with red stars, and then unfold.

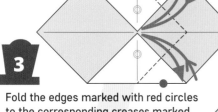

Step 3 is complete.

Turn over

Step 4 is folded in this way. Make sure to make creases only where marked with red stars, and open back out.

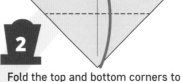

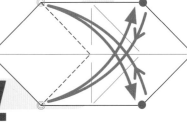

4

Once you have turned it over top to bottom, fold so the corners marked with double circles meet those with red circles as shown to make 2 more creases.

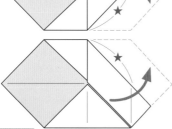

In the corresponding video, this is titled "Peek-a-Boo Ghost."

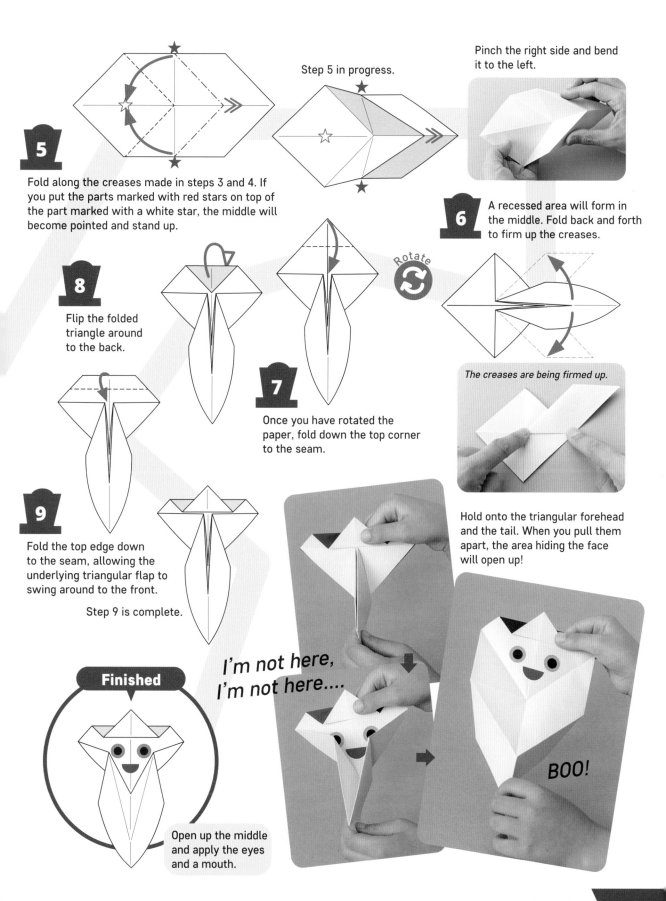

5

Fold along the creases made in steps 3 and 4. If you put the parts marked with red stars on top of the part marked with a white star, the middle will become pointed and stand up.

Step 5 in progress.

Pinch the right side and bend it to the left.

6

A recessed area will form in the middle. Fold back and forth to firm up the creases.

Rotate

The creases are being firmed up.

8

Flip the folded triangle around to the back.

7

Once you have rotated the paper, fold down the top corner to the seam.

Hold onto the triangular forehead and the tail. When you pull them apart, the area hiding the face will open up!

9

Fold the top edge down to the seam, allowing the underlying triangular flap to swing around to the front.

Step 9 is complete.

I'm not here, I'm not here....

Finished

Open up the middle and apply the eyes and a mouth.

BOO!

Tombstone

It's creepy, but it's just a gravestone, right? But it occasionally wobbles around on its own, so maybe it's haunted!

Practicality	★ ★
Endurance	★ ★ ★ ★ ★
Price	★ ★
Characteristics	It inexplicably moves of its own accord.

VIDEO
Type this URL into your browser:
tuttlepublishing.com/
origami-monsters
-and-magic

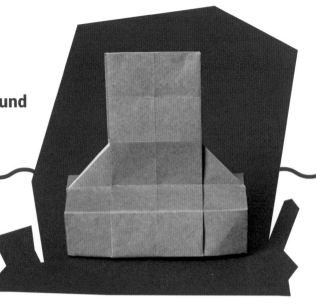

Basic Shape Fold a 16-Row Precrease (see page 125).

Pinch just one square each.

3

Once you have turned it over, pinch the places marked with red stars from the back and make 4 short creases.

Turn over

Step 2 is complete.

1

Unfold completely. Pinch out the two lines on top and bottom marked with red stars into mountain folds, and fold them in to the center point marked with a white star.

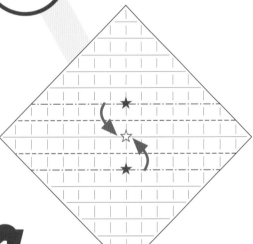

Step 1 in progress.

2

Pinch out the two creases on the left and right marked with red stars into mountain folds, and fold them in to the center point marked with a white star.

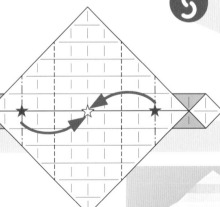

Step 2 in progress.

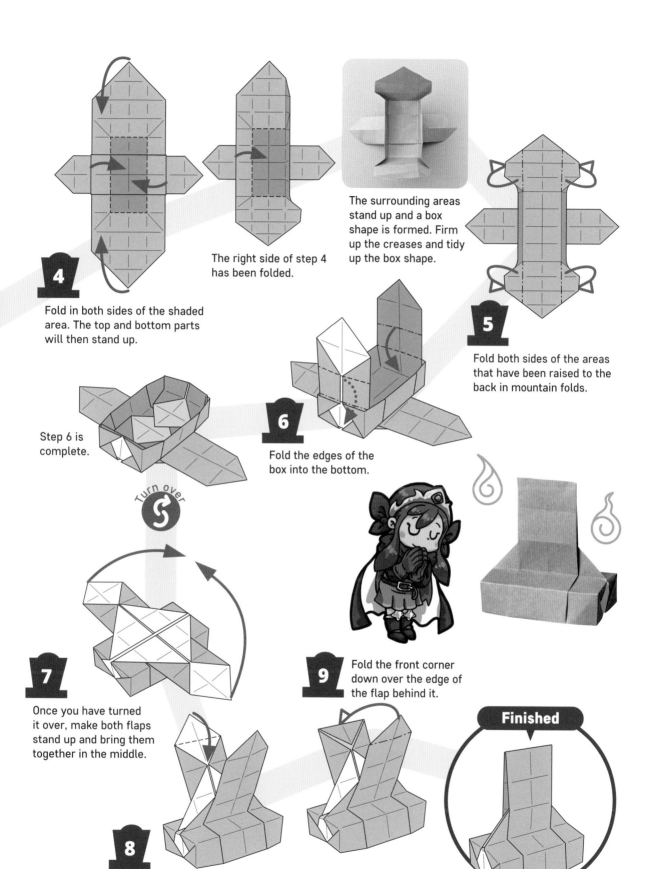

4

Fold in both sides of the shaded area. The top and bottom parts will then stand up.

The right side of step 4 has been folded.

The surrounding areas stand up and a box shape is formed. Firm up the creases and tidy up the box shape.

5

Fold both sides of the areas that have been raised to the back in mountain folds.

Step 6 is complete.

6

Fold the edges of the box into the bottom.

Turn over

7

Once you have turned it over, make both flaps stand up and bring them together in the middle.

9

Fold the front corner down over the edge of the flap behind it.

Finished

8

Fold the back corner in to the inside.

Jaw-Dropping Skull

The jaw of this skull suddenly drops. It's an alarming yet comical phantom.

Attack Power	★★
Defense Power	★★★★
Mystical Power	★★
Special Abilities	Can detach its jaw. Adept at giving people a fright.

VIDEO
Type this URL into your browser:
tuttlepublishing.com/origami-monsters-and-magic

Basic Shape   Fold a 16-Row Precrease (see page 125).

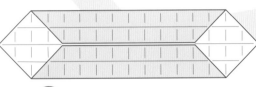

1   Open up the top and bottom rows to form this shape.

2   Once you have turned it over, fold the left and right corners in along the dashed crease lines.

Step 3 is complete.

3   Fold in another column on the left and 2 columns on the right.

4   Once you have turned it over top to bottom, fold all 4 corners into triangles.

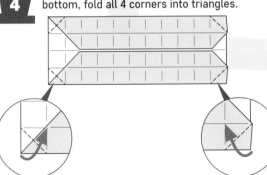

5   Fold the top and bottom edges to the center line.

In the corresponding video, this is titled "Jaw Down Scull."

The Noodle-Necked Monster is on page 76, and the Wobbly Zombie is on page 84.

It's the Ghostly Trio!

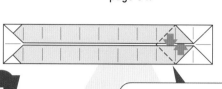

6

A close-up of the right side. Insert your fingers where indicated by the squat arrows, and spread out the paper in the directions of the long arrows.

7

The right side is standing up. Push it toward the left and flatten it.

8

Spread open the inside of the left side in the same way as step 6 and spread out the paper in the directions of the long arrows.

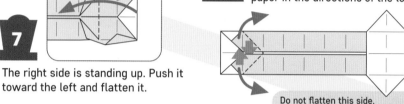

Do not flatten this side.

Step 8 is complete. Do not flatten the left side, but keep it standing up.

9

Once you have turned it over, fold the right side in to swivel the white hexagon to the front.

Turn over

10

Alternate between mountain folds and valley folds along the existing creases to make a zig-zag shape.

Squeeze down the zig-zagged part and hold onto the skull. When you release the jaw, it drops!

11

Slightly fold back both triangular flaps of the hexagon shape with mountain folds.

Rotate

Finished

Draw on the face and teeth.

DROP!

Wobbly Zombie

A shambling corpse that wanders unsteadily around the graveyard with its hands held out. Its movements are slow, but relentless.

Attack Power	★ ★ ★
Defense Power	★ ★ ★ ★
Mystical Power	★ ★ ★ ★
Special Abilities	Because it is undead, its uncoordinated movements are difficult to anticipate.

VIDEO
Type this URL into your browser:
tuttlepublishing.com/ origami-monsters -and-magic

Basic Shape Fold an 8-Row Precrease (2) (see page 124).

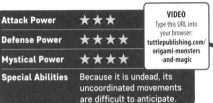

1 Insert your fingers where indicated by the squat arrows, 3 squares from the right. Open the paper up in the directions of the long arrows.

2 Once the right part has raised up, push it down to the left side and flatten it.

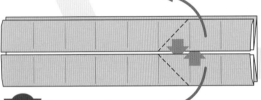

3 Insert your fingers where indicated by the squat arrows, and spread out the corners.

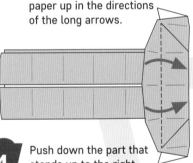

4 Push down the part that stands up to the right, and press it flat.

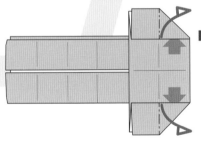

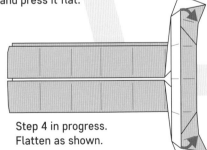

Step 4 in progress. Flatten as shown.

5 Fold back the top and bottom ends to the right along the dashed lines.

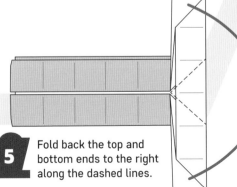

In the corresponding video, this is titled "Staggering Zombie."

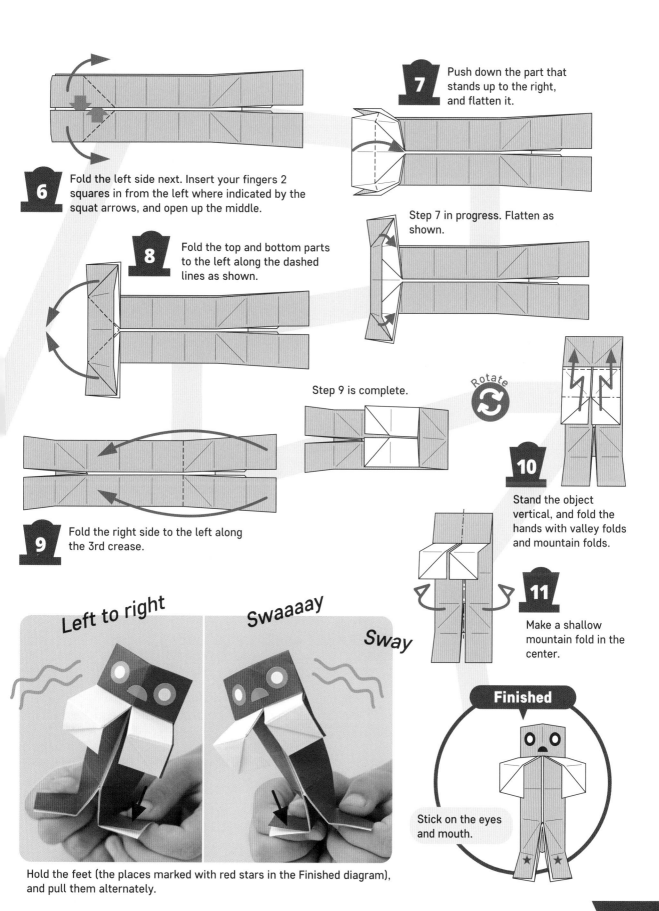

6 Fold the left side next. Insert your fingers 2 squares in from the left where indicated by the squat arrows, and open up the middle.

7 Push down the part that stands up to the right, and flatten it.

Step 7 in progress. Flatten as shown.

8 Fold the top and bottom parts to the left along the dashed lines as shown.

Step 9 is complete.

Rotate

9 Fold the right side to the left along the 3rd crease.

10 Stand the object vertical, and fold the hands with valley folds and mountain folds.

11 Make a shallow mountain fold in the center.

Finished

Stick on the eyes and mouth.

Left to right

Swaaaay

Sway

Hold the feet (the places marked with red stars in the Finished diagram), and pull them alternately.

The Grim Reaper

The Grim Reaper appears at the side of people who are about to die, ready to whisk their souls away. If you see it, prepare yourself, because your time is just about up!

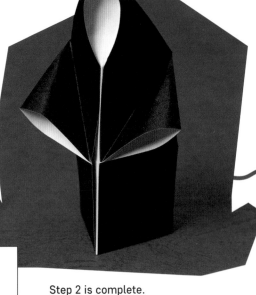

Attack Power	★★★★
Defense Power	★★★★
Mystical Power	★★★★★
Special Abilities	Reaps a soul with one swipe of its large scythe (page 88).

VIDEO
Type this URL into your browser:
tuttlepublishing.com/origami-monsters-and-magic

1 Fold the paper in half edge to edge both ways and unfold to make 2 creases.

2 Fold in the left and right edges to the center line.

Step 2 is complete.

Turn over

3 Once you have turned it over, fold up the bottom edge to the center line.

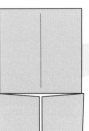
Step 3 is complete.

Turn over

4 Once you have turned it over left to right, fold down the top edge to the crease, and then unfold.

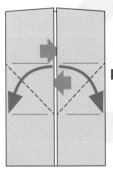

5 Insert your fingers where indicated by the squat arrows, and fold diagonally to the bottom to open up the middle.

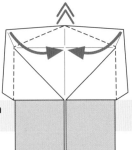

6 Fold diagonally from both sides and make the part marked with double arrows pointed, and flatten.

In the corresponding video, this is titled "Death."

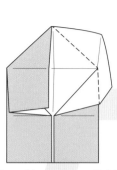

Step 6 in progress. Fold the right side in the same way.

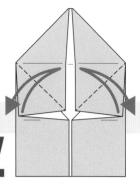

7

Fold the corners that are formed into triangles, and then unfold.

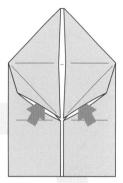

8

Insert your fingers into the pockets where indicated by squat arrows, and puff them up. These will become the sleeves.

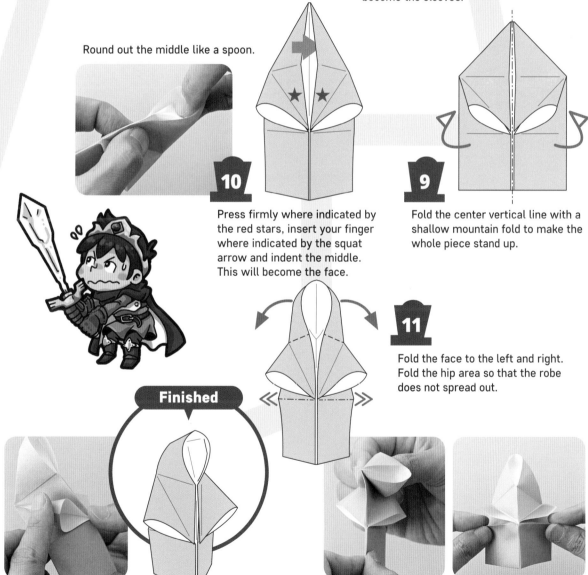

Round out the middle like a spoon.

10

Press firmly where indicated by the red stars, insert your finger where indicated by the squat arrow and indent the middle. This will become the face.

9

Fold the center vertical line with a shallow mountain fold to make the whole piece stand up.

11

Fold the face to the left and right. Fold the hip area so that the robe does not spread out.

Finished

Gently press above the crease to round out the sleeves.

Make a firm crease at the base of the neck.

Pinch the hip part and make a mountain fold.

Reaper's Scythe

It is said that when the Grim Reaper's gigantic, gleaming blade slashes down, it always reaps a soul.

Practicality	★ ★ ★ ★
Magic Power	★ ★ ★ ★ ★
Price	?????
Characteristics	Well-sharpened, its keen edge is unparalleled.

VIDEO
Type this URL into your browser:
tuttlepublishing.com/
origami-monsters
-and-magic

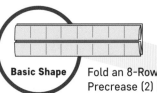

Basic Shape

Fold an 8-Row Precrease (2) (see page 124).

1
Insert your fingers where indicated by the squat arrows, 4 squares from the left. Open the paper up in the directions of the long arrows.

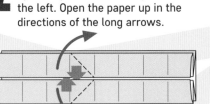

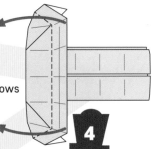

2
Push down the part that stands up, and flatten it.

6
Turn one column of the edge to the back.

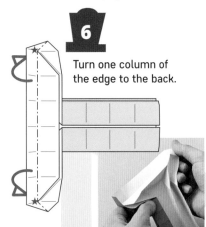

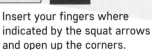

3
Insert your fingers where indicated by the squat arrows and open up the corners.

4
Push down the part that stands up on the left, and flatten it.

Hold onto the places marked with red stars in the diagram and turn the paper inside out.

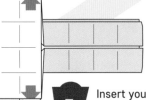

5
Insert your fingers where indicated by the squat arrows and open up the corners.

7
Fold in the bottom corner.

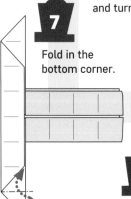

8
Fold the whole object in half, and insert both of the corners marked with a red star into the pocket marked with a white star.

Step 8 is complete.

Turn over 🔄

Finished

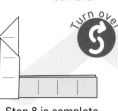

Squawking Crow

The crow's endless cawing is raucous. It's just a small creature, but it will reveal your location to the dreaded Grim Reaper, so chase it off quickly.

Attack Power	★
Defense Power	★ ★
Mystical Power	★
Special Abilities	Tattling, backbiting and gossiping.

VIDEO
Type this URL into your browser:
tuttlepublishing.com/ origami-monsters -and-magic

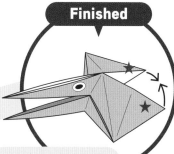

Basic Shape

Fold a Fish Base (see page 126).

1 Open up the top layer on the right to the left.

2 Fold the edges marked with red circles to meet the crease marked with a double circle to make 2 creases.

Step 2 is folded in this way. Make creases only where marked with red stars, and then unfold.

3 Make creases in the same way as step 2 on the left side.

4 Pinch the corners marked with double arrows and fold the piece in half to make the beak. The diamond-shaped area in the middle (shaded) will become indented.

Step 4 in progress.

Rotate

5 Push the beak flaps toward the sides, and firm up the creases.

The pocket in the middle has been opened up.

6 Once you have turned the beak flaps to the other side, insert your fingers in the pocket in the back indicated by squat arrows and open up the middle.

Finished

Stick on the eyes. If you move the parts marked with red stars, the beak will open and close.

In the corresponding video, this is titled "Noisy Crow."

The Face of Dracula

A vampire that bites unsuspecting travelers on the neck to drink their blood. They dislike sunlight and crucifixes. You can defeat them if you put a wooden stake through them.

Attack Power	★★★★	
Defense Power	★★★	
Mystical Power	★★★	
Special Abilities	Bites suddenly to consume your blood.	

VIDEO
Type this URL into your browser:
tuttlepublishing.com/origami-monsters-and-magic

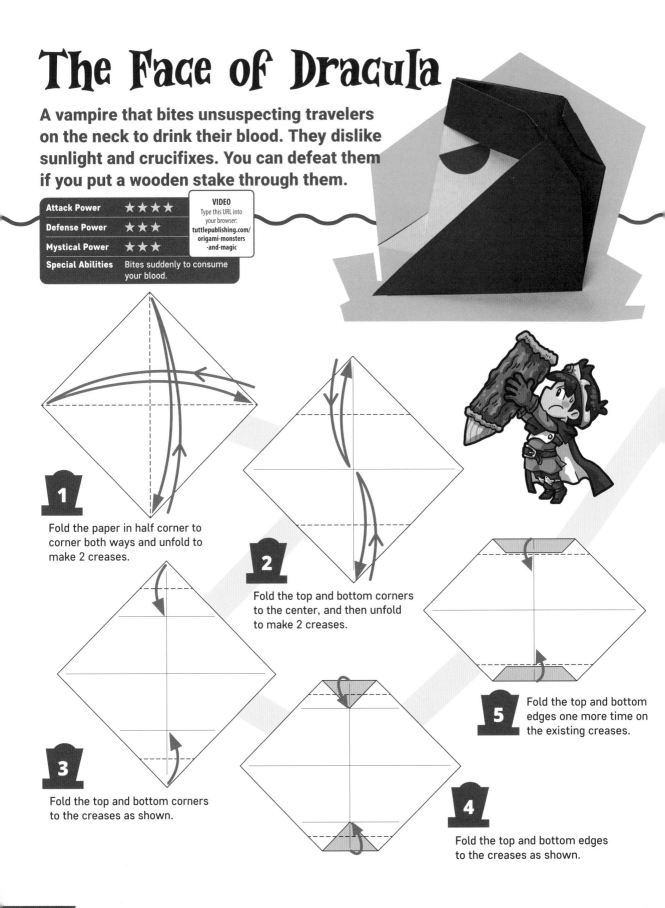

1 Fold the paper in half corner to corner both ways and unfold to make 2 creases.

2 Fold the top and bottom corners to the center, and then unfold to make 2 creases.

3 Fold the top and bottom corners to the creases as shown.

4 Fold the top and bottom edges to the creases as shown.

5 Fold the top and bottom edges one more time on the existing creases.

In the corresponding video, this is titled "Biting Man."

Fold the right corner about ⅓ inch (1 cm) to the left of the center line.

Fold the left corner about ⅓ inch (1 cm) to the right of the center line in the same way.

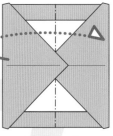

8
Make a mountain fold in the vertical center. The corners folded in steps 6 and 7 will become the mouth. Leave them sticking out.

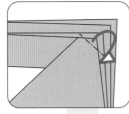

10
This is a close-up of the top right corner. Fold the first layer into a small mountain fold and tuck it in.

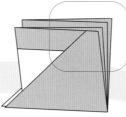
Step 9 is complete. From this point on, the indicated corner (which will become the head) will be folded.

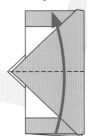

9
Fold through the middle horizontally.

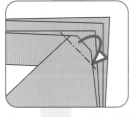

11
Make another small mountain fold.

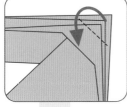

12
Fold in the next 2 layers into a small valley fold.

BITE!

Pull on the area marked with a red star in the Finished diagram (the section where two layers have been folded together). As soon as you release it, the head will bite.

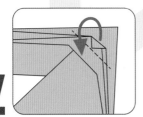

13
Narrowly fold the corner you just folded once again.

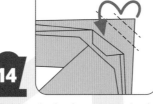

14
Fold in the back corner twice in the same way.

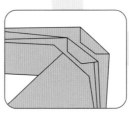
Step 14 is complete.

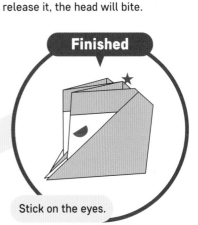

Finished

Stick on the eyes.

Crucifix

A potent symbol that helps you defeat monsters with its supernatural power. When you hold it up, enemies will flee.

Practicality	★★★★
Endurance	★★★
Price	★★★★★
Characteristics	Its beautiful form conceals otherworldly power.

VIDEO
Type this URL into your browser:
tuttlepublishing.com/origami-monsters-and-magic

Basic Shape

Fold a Balloon Base (see page 126).

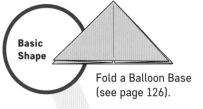

1 Fold the entire shape in half horizontally, and then unfold to make a crease. Press the crease very firmly.

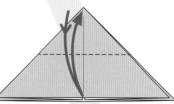

2 Fold the top and bottom to the crease made in step 1, and make 2 more creases.

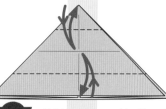

3 3 creases have been made. Unfold the entire paper.

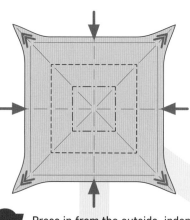

5 Press in from the outside, indent the valley folds and make the mountain folds stick up.

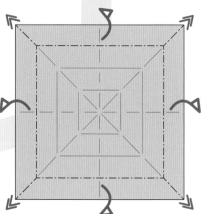

4 There is a series of concentric square creases. Pinch the corners marked with double arrows, and make mountain folds on the outermost creases.

Make the middle indented.

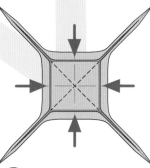

6 4 thin horns have been created. Press and flatten one more time from the outside of the center part and make the valley folds indented.

In the corresponding video, this is titled "Cross."

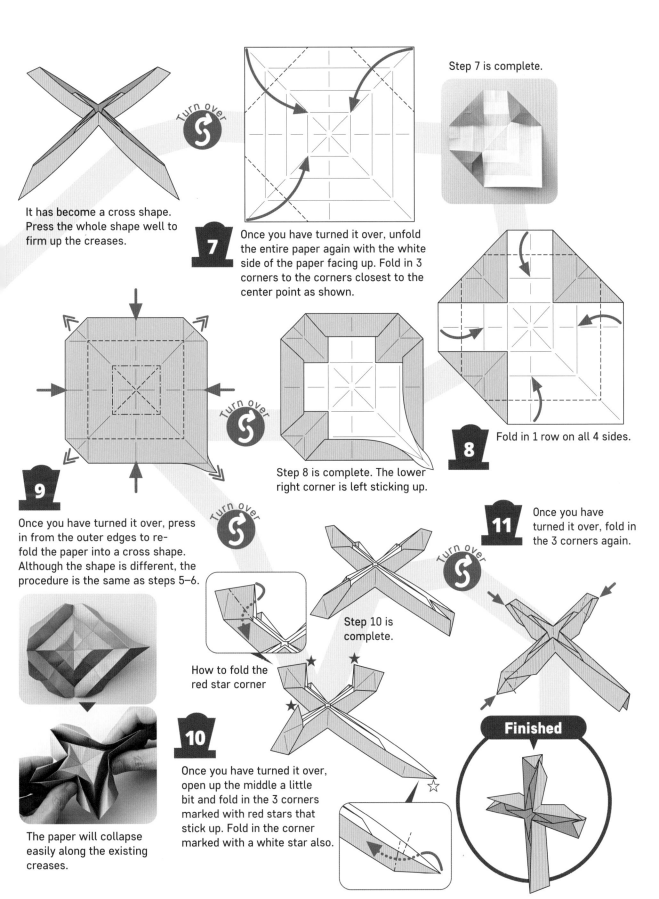

It has become a cross shape. Press the whole shape well to firm up the creases.

7 Once you have turned it over, unfold the entire paper again with the white side of the paper facing up. Fold in 3 corners to the corners closest to the center point as shown.

Step 7 is complete.

8 Fold in 1 row on all 4 sides.

Step 8 is complete. The lower right corner is left sticking up.

9 Once you have turned it over, press in from the outer edges to re-fold the paper into a cross shape. Although the shape is different, the procedure is the same as steps 5–6.

The paper will collapse easily along the existing creases.

Step 10 is complete.

How to fold the red star corner

10 Once you have turned it over, open up the middle a little bit and fold in the 3 corners marked with red stars that stick up. Fold in the corner marked with a white star also.

11 Once you have turned it over, fold in the 3 corners again.

Finished

Disguise Item (1)

Pop-Out Eyeballs

Transform yourself into a strange denizen of the magic world with a disguise! First, use bulging eyeballs that pop-out in surprise to make you look like a character best to be avoided!

Degree of Origami Magic Involved	★ ★ ★ ★ ★
Entertainment Value	★ ★ ★ ★ ★
Tip	Using this prop takes skill, so be sure to practice.

VIDEO
Type this URL into your browser:
tuttlepublishing.com/
origami-monsters
-and-magic

Step 5 is complete.

Basic Shape   Fold a 16-Row Precrease (see page 125).

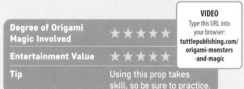

1   Fold out one row each on the top and bottom to form this shape.

Turn over

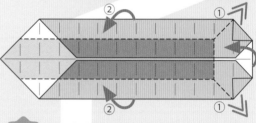

5   Pinch the corners marked with double arrows from the back and make diagonal creases. If you lift up the places marked (1) and (2), the paper around the shaded area will stand up.

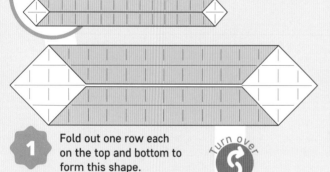

2   Once you have turned it over, fold in the right corner along the first crease.

Turn over

Step 4 is complete.

3   Fold in the right side again, 2 squares in from the first fold as shown.

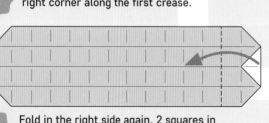

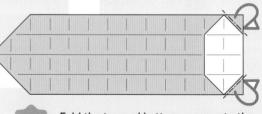

4   Fold the top and bottom corners to the back with mountain folds. Press hard.

In the corresponding video, this is titled "Coming Off Eyes."

This hexagon will be white.

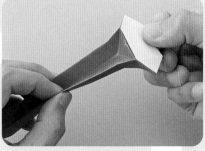

Turn over

6 Once you have turned it over, press the sides into valley folds and collapse them. The part marked with a red star will become a triangular recessed area.

If you press in both sides, the base of the white of the eye will become indented into a triangular shape.

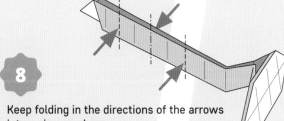

7 Fold the base of the white of the eye into a valley fold, and fold the next segment into a mountain fold.

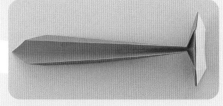

Step 6 is complete.

The zig-zag parts are springs, so fold them in and hold the eyeballs against your closed eyelids. Be sure to close your eyes firmly first so that the origami papers and your fingers don't get into them!

8 Keep folding in the directions of the arrows into a zig-zag shape.

9 The right eye has been completed. For the left eye, fold the zig-zag shape in the opposite directions, in mirror image.

Finished

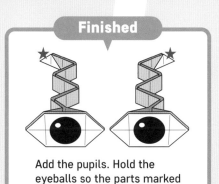

Add the pupils. Hold the eyeballs so the parts marked with red stars face outward.

SPRRRING!

Were you surprised?

Disguise Item (2)

Fake Mustache

He's not a monster, but if you think of characters with mustaches, you have to think of Mario! If you put on a mustache yourself, you'll feel like a big shot.

Degree of Origami Magic Involved	★ ★
Entertainment Value	★ ★ ★ ★
Tip	Hold the projecting tab between your lips, and curl or twirl the mustache ends.

VIDEO
Type this URL into your browser:
tuttlepublishing.com/ origami-monsters -and-magic

1 Fold the paper in half corner to corner both ways and unfold to make 2 creases.

2 Fold the top corner behind to the center line, and fold the bottom corner in to the front center line.

3 Fold the edges marked with red circles to meet the crease marked with a double circle to make 2 diagonal creases. Unfold.

In the corresponding video, this is titled "'Wearable' Mustache."

4 Fold the upper part in the same way as step 3, putting together the edges marked with red circles and the crease marked with a double circle to make 2 diagonal creases. Unfold.

5 If you fold in all 4 corners, the left and right corners will stand up like horns.

Step 6 is complete.

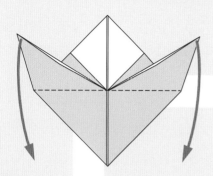

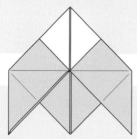

Turn over

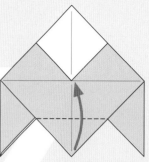

6 Fold down the horns that stand up.

7 Once you have turned it over, fold up the bottom corner to the center.

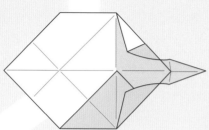

8

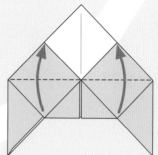

Fold up the upper layer of the bottom part at the crease as shown.

Step 5 in progress.

Rotate Turn over

Step 8 is complete.

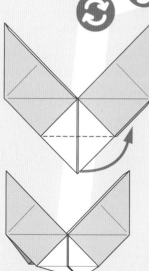

9 Once you have turned it over and rotated it, fold up the lower corner so that it stands perpendicular to the plane of the rest of the model.

AHEM!

UH-HUH!

AWESOME TIME

Step 9 is complete.

Turn over

Finished

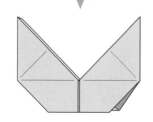

Hold the white triangle that you folded in step 9 with your mouth.

Disguise Item (3)

Wagging Tongue

The third magic disguise item is one that transforms you into a slobbering monster. You "shake hands" with your tongue, and then, of course, there's the "high five"....

Degree of Origami Magic Involved	★ ★ ★ ★
Entertainment Value	★ ★ ★ ★ ★
Tip	Move it skillfully with your mouth. Using double-sided origami paper will make this item look even more realistic.

VIDEO
Type this URL into your browser:
tuttlepublishing.com/origami-monsters-and-magic

1 Fold the paper in half corner to corner both ways and unfold to make 2 creases.

2 Fold the right corner to the center point and unfold to make a crease.

3 Fold in the right corner to the first crease.

4 Fold in again at the crease.

5 Fold in the paper at the edge of the part you just folded and unfold to make a crease.

Step 5 is complete.

Turn over

6 Once you have turned it over, fold in the top and bottom corners to the center line.

In the corresponding video, this is titled "Licking Tongue."

8

Insert your fingers where indicated by the squat arrows, and open up the middle in the direction of the long arrows.

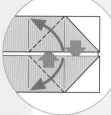

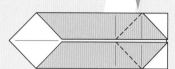

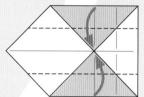

7

Fold the top and bottom edges down to the center line.

9

Make firm creases where marked by red stars, and open up to the top and bottom.

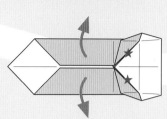

The bottom is being opened up and folded up. Press flat.

10

Make a mountain fold at the crease indicated by a dashed line, and fold to the back.

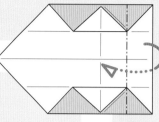

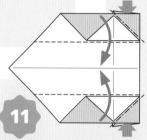

11

Insert your fingers where indicated by squat arrows and open up those places. Then, fold in the top and bottom edges to the center line.

12

Fold a little of the tip of the tongue.

Rotate

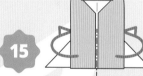

Step 11 is complete.

13

Wrap the tongue around a pencil or similar tool to curl it.

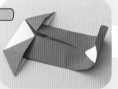

Curl it up about as shown in the photo.

Turn over

14

After you have turned it over, fold the tongue up at the base.

15

Fold in the sides of only the lower half of the tongue with a mountain fold to the back.

Press firmly to make a fold where marked by the red star, and then lower the tongue.

Finished

Play with the tongue by holding onto the places marked with red stars in the Finished diagram. Every time you move your fingers together and apart, the tongue will move up and down.

BLAAAHH!

99

Were you able to defeat
the Cemetery monsters!?

We're finally on the last stage!

Cemetery

5 SHOWDOWN IN THE DUNGEON

The dark dungeon is full of eerie monsters you've never seen before. Clear the dragon waiting at the end to obtain the treasure!

Creepy Hands

Something sticky touched me in
the dark.... Waaahh! Ewww!
A monster with hands only!?

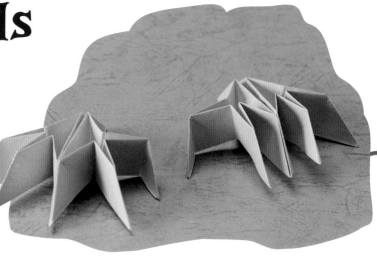

Attack Power	★
Defense Power	★
Magic Power	★★
Characteristics	Misleads people with magic. Skitters fast.

VIDEO
Type this URL into
your browser:
**tuttlepublishing.com/
origami-monsters
-and-magic**

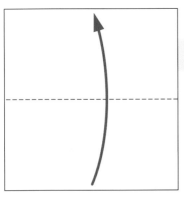

1 Fold in half.

Turn over

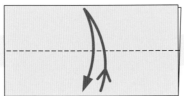

2 Fold in half again
and unfold to make a
crease.

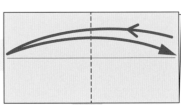

3 Fold in half vertically and
unfold to make a crease.

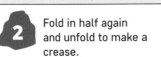

Step 4 is complete.

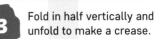

4 Fold in the left and right
sides and unfold to make 2
creases.

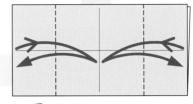

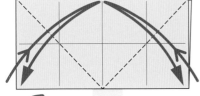

5 Once you have turned it over left to
right, fold the bottom 2 corners to the
top to make 2 diagonal creases.

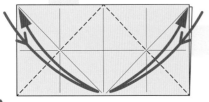

6 Next, fold down the 2 top
corners to the bottom to make
2 more diagonal creases.

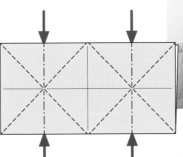

The right side X is being indented.

7 Press the places marked with arrows
from the back to indent the X's.

In the corresponding video, this is titled "Scary Hand 2."

In addition to the X creases, 2 square creases have been created.

11 We'll start by pinching on the right half. Fold at the dashed mountain creases once, pinch the corners marked with double arrows, and press in from the top and bottom.

10 Spread back out to the step 7 stage.

13 The right side has been pressed into an X shape. Fold the left half in the same way as steps 11–12.

9 Fold in the left and right corners to the center to make 2 creases.

12 Keep pressing, and indent the X inside of the smaller square.

Little finger

14 Fold the right hand. Fold the thumb twice, and fold the little finger once to the back side.

Thumb

Finished

The right hand is complete. When folding the left hand, fold it in mirror image to step 14.

8 Fold in the sides and flatten.

SKITTER———

Tap the wrist with your finger. The hand will skitter forward.

Chattering Teeth

A monster consisting of only a mouth that clacks its jaws while biting you. If you hear a ghastly sound in the darkness, be ready!

Attack Power	★ ★ ★
Defense Power	★
Magic Power	★
Characteristics	Its weakness is that it has no sense of direction, because it has no eyes.

VIDEO
Type this URL into your browser:
tuttlepublishing.com/origami-monsters-and-magic

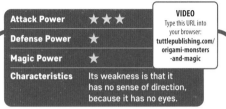

Basic Shape Fold an 8-Row Precrease (2) (see page 124).

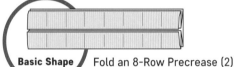

1 Make 4 diagonal creases in the center 4 squares.

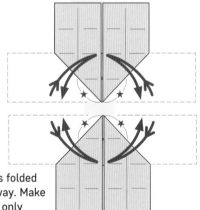

Step 1 is folded in this way. Make creases only where marked with red stars.

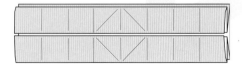

Step 1 is complete.

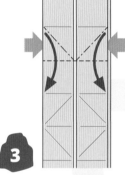

3 Insert your fingers from both sides, open toward the direction of the arrow, and flatten.

Step 3 in progress. After inserting your finger to spread the paper, squash it flat.

Rotate

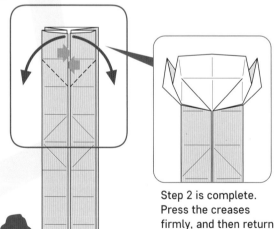

Step 2 is complete. Press the creases firmly, and then return to the original state.

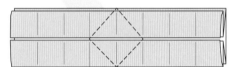

2 Change the direction and fold the upper part. Insert your fingers where indicated by the squat arrows, and fold down diagonally to spread out the middle.

In the corresponding video, this is titled "Biting Mouth."

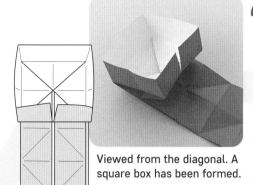

Viewed from the diagonal. A square box has been formed.

Step 3 is complete.

4 Turn the lower right corner of the box marked with a red star inside out, and press it into the upper right corner.

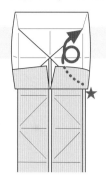

Step 4 in progress. Start by firmly holding onto the red-star-marked corner from the outside.

Press your thumb in and turn the paper over, and insert into the upper right corner.

5 Fold the lower left corner marked with a red star in the same way. Fold the other end in the same way too, following the directions from steps 2–5.

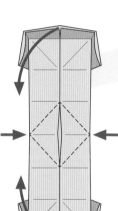

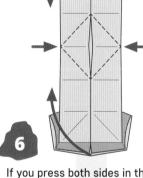

6 If you press both sides in the middle, the upper and lower ends will stand up to form the mouth.

If you press from both sides, the mouth will close and make a sound!

CLACK CLACK CLACK!

Finished

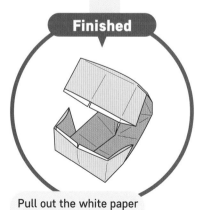

Pull out the white paper a bit to form the teeth.

Viewed from the back. Hold the jaw from both sides.

Flaming Torch

We finally got our hands on a torch! Now we aren't afraid of the dark anymore! (Although the monsters are still scary.)

Convenience	★ ★ ★ ★ ★
Durability	★ ★ ★
Price	★ ★
Characteristics	The brightness of the torch changes with the magic power of the bearer.

VIDEO
Type this URL into your browser:
tuttlepublishing.com/
origami-monsters
-and-magic

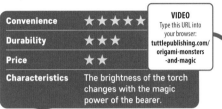

Basic Shape — Fold a 16-Row Precrease (see page 125).

2 Pinch the crease marked with the red star into a mountain fold, and align the fold with the crease marked with a white star in the same way as step 1.

1 Unfold completely and position the colored side facing up. Pinch the crease marked with a red star into a mountain fold, and align the fold with the crease marked with a white star.

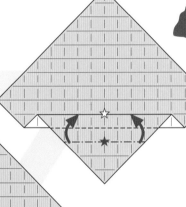

3 Repeat step 2 for the crease marked with a red star, folding it up to the crease with a white star.

Step 4 is folded in this way. Make short creases only where marked by the red star and unfold.

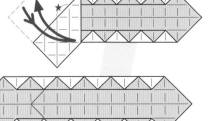

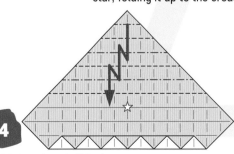

4 Fold the upper half in the same way as steps 1–3.

5 Make 2 diagonal creases where marked by red lines.

In the corresponding video, this is titled "Torch."

6 Fold in the right corner at the 2nd crease.

7 Fold in the right side at the 5th crease.

9 Once you have turned it over, slightly fold up the top and bottom edges at the dashed lines.

Turn over

8 Make 2 short diagonal creases where marked by red lines.

Step 8 is complete.

Fold step 8 in this way. Make short creases only where marked by red stars, and open back up.

10 Push up the mountain crease in the middle, while pushing in the sides at the same time. Push the middle toward the left, and the triangle in the center marked with a red star will pop up.

The part marked with a black line is the triangular area defined by the red star in the diagram.

11 Fold the left side in the same way as step 10, to make the triangle marked with a white star pop up.

Pinch from both sides, and then push your left and right hands together.

Finished

Turn over   Rotate

The flame part has been spread out.

12 Insert your fingers where marked by squat arrows and open up the middle to form a flame shape.

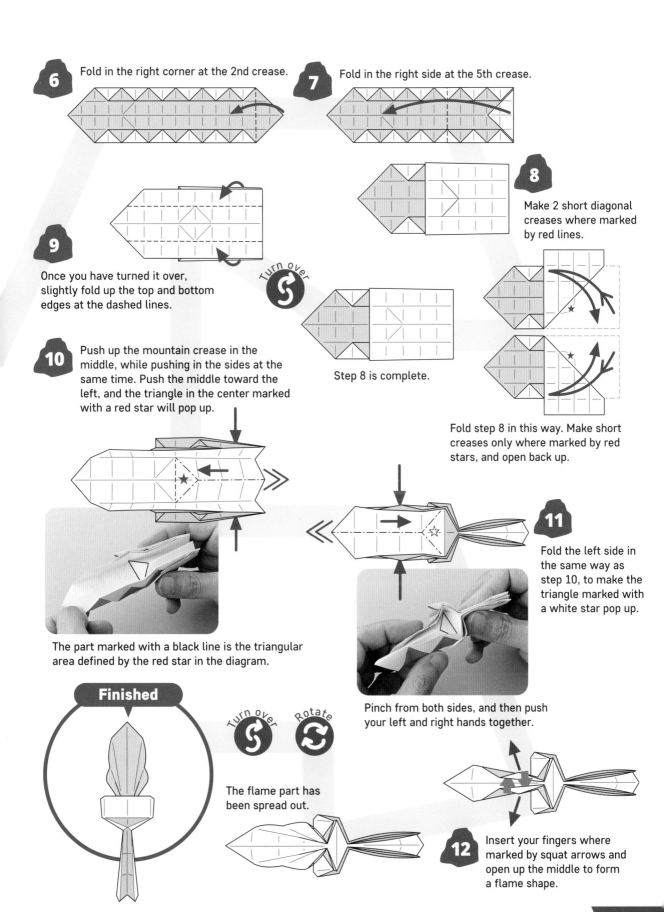

Flapping Bat

It senses intruders, and attacks while flapping its big wings. You'll want to take care not to be surrounded by a horde of them.

Attack Power	★ ★
Defense Power	★ ★ ★
Magic Power	★ ★
Special Abilities	Ultrasonic attack that is focused by its large wings.

VIDEO
Type this URL into your browser:
tuttlepublishing.com/origami-monsters-and-magic

Basic Shape

Fold a Blintz Base (see page 123).

Rotate

Step 1 is complete.

Turn over

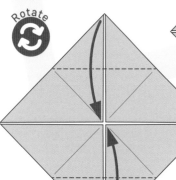

1

Fold the top and bottom corners to the center.

Step 2 in progress.

2

Once you have turned it over, bring up the edges marked with red circles to meet the creases marked with double circles to make new creases, and unfold.

3

Bring down the upper diagonal edges marked with red circles to meet the creases marked with double circles to make new creases, and unfold.

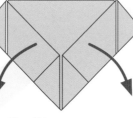

4

Fold in the sides of the shaded square in the center. The left and right points will stand up like horns.

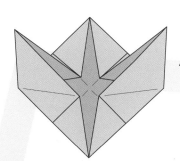

Step 4 is complete. Firm up the creases at the bases of the horns.

Turn over

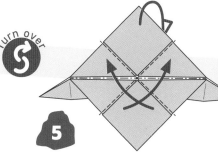

5 Once you have turned it over, make 2 diagonal valley creases and 1 horizontal mountain crease in the middle, where indicated.

When making the crease in the middle, fold the entire object in half into a mountain fold.

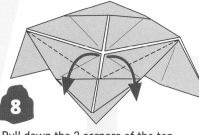

8 Pull down the 2 corners of the top layer of the bottom half.

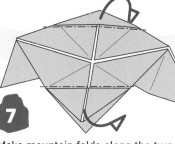

7 Make mountain folds along the two creases folded in step 6, and unfold.

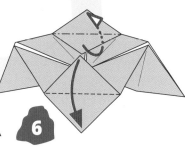

6 Fold down the bottom corner to the outside and the top corner to the inside.

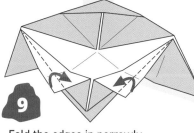

9 Fold the edges in narrowly.

10 Fold the corners formed in step 9 into triangles and make then stand up. These are the ears. Make the corner in the front stand up too, to form the nose.

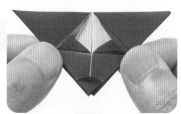

11 Push the wings to the center and firm up the creases.

If you hold the places marked with red stars in the Finished diagram and pull to the front and back, the wings will flap.

Finished

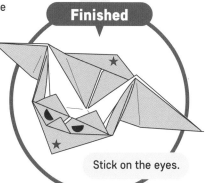

Stick on the eyes.

Whispering Imp

Whispers directly to the minds of travelers, and makes them lose the will to fight in the dungeon. Its utterances are mostly lies.

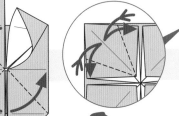

Attack Power	★★
Defense Power	★★★★
Magic Power	★★★★★
Special Abilities	The whispers of this imp are very dark indeed.

VIDEO
Type this URL into your browser:
tuttlepublishing.com/origami-monsters-and-magic

Basic Shape

Fold a Boat Base (see page 123).

1
Insert your fingers where indicated by the squat arrow, and press down and out into a square shape.

Step 1 in progress. Flatten the other 3 areas in the same way.

2
Fold in both sides of the 4 squares folded in step 1 on the dashed lines toward the center lines as shown to make creases. Unfold.

3
Open up the corner. Flatten into a diamond shape.

The diamond shape in step 3 is being folded and flattened. Fold and flatten the other 3 corners in the same way.

4
Swing down the top corner, and fold the left and right corners into half.

Step 3 is complete.

Rotate

Pull the places marked with red stars in the Finished diagram, and make the mouth move.

Finished

Stick on the eyes.

5
If you pinch the 2 places marked with red stars and pull them out to the sides, the snout will drop down.

In the corresponding video, this is titled "Biting Devil."

Deadly Spider

Its venom is deadly, so whatever you do, do not get bitten by it! The spider's web is strong enough to even entangle humans.

Attack Power	★ ★ ★ ★
Defense Power	★ ★ ★
Magic Power	★ ★ ★
Special Abilities	Its very venomous bite and the sticky threads of its web.

VIDEO
Type this URL into your browser:
tuttlepublishing.com/ origami-monsters -and-magic

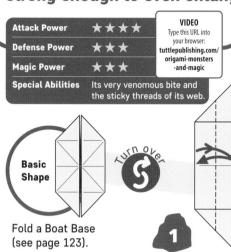

Basic Shape

Fold a Boat Base (see page 123).

Turn over

1
Once you have turned it over, fold in the left and right sides to the center to make creases. Unfold.

2
Bring the corners marked with double circles to meet the edges marked with red circles to make creases. Unfold.

Step 2 is folded in this way.

5
Make a vertical mountain fold in the middle, and fold everything in half.

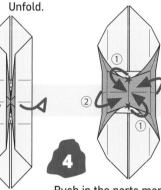

4
Push in the parts marked with red stars to the center, and then make the left and right sides overlap as you flatten everything.

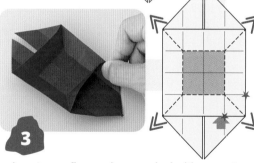

3
Insert your finger where marked with a squat arrow, put the two red stars together and make a short diagonal mountain fold. Repeat in all 4 corners, and the shaded middle square will stand up.

6
Insert your fingers where indicated by squat arrows, and spread out to the outside. Do the same on the left side.

Turn over

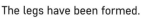

The legs have been formed.

Finished

Poke from the back to make it jump.

In the corresponding video, this is titled "Jumping Spider."

Infernal Dragon

The last-stage monster has finally appeared!
Whatever you do, avoid its fiery breath.
Fight this monster with all your might!

Attack Power	★ ★ ★ ★ ★
Defense Power	★ ★ ★ ★ ★
Magic Power	★ ★ ★ ★ ★
Special Abilities	Bone-melting fire fanned by powerful wings.

VIDEO
Type this URL into your browser:
tuttlepublishing.com/origami-monsters-and-magic

Basic Shape

Fold a Crane Base (see page 127).

Rotate

1 Rotate 180°, and fold up both of the bottom corners.

Step 1 is complete.

2 Viewed diagonally. Open up the front and back sides.

3 Pull firmly until the bottom becomes flat.

Press flat little by little from both sides and the front.

4 Collapse the triangle that is sticking up in the front. Press down on the 3 parts marked with red stars to flatten it.

When you pull both sides, it forms this shape.

Make the center firmly pointed.

Step 4 is complete. Flatten the triangle in the back in the same way.

5 Exercise the creases at the bases of the perpendicular triangular flaps by folding to both sides. Then, fold the flaps down to the right.

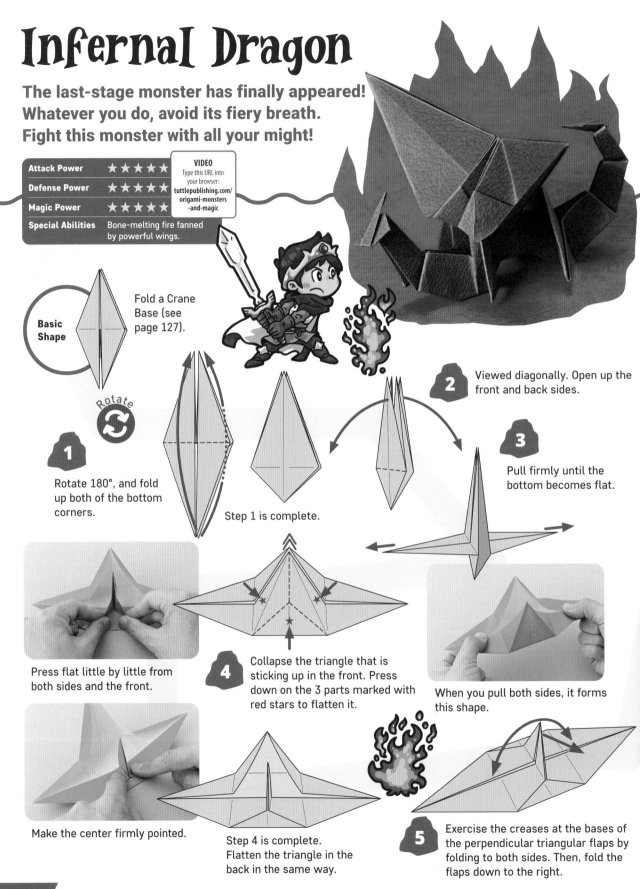

In the corresponding video, this is titled "Dragon."

6

Once you have turned it over, make 2 creases in an X shape as shown.

Turn over

Step 5 is complete.

Step 6 is folded in this way. Make firm creases where marked with red stars and open back out.

Pull out the triangular flap from behind and crease along the indicated line.

Step 7 in progress.

7

Pinch out the corners marked with double arrows into a mountain fold, and bring the mountain fold together to the front. The X creases will become indented.

Rotate

If you bring together the left and right corners in the front, it will form this shape.

Viewed from below, the neck and tail are flat.

9

Fold the neck and tail in half to make them thin, and then unfold.

8

The object has been flattened and is being viewed from the top. Pull out the lower corners with inside reverse folds. These parts will become the neck and tail.

Step 11 is complete.

10

Use the creases to fold in the corners marked with red stars to the inside.

★   ★

11

Lift up the corners and flatten the bottom.

Continues ➡

Infernal Dragon

Viewed from below

Neck   Tail

13

Press the neck and tail in half with a valley fold.

Rotate

These will become the wings

12 Make 1 small step fold on the neck and 3 small step folds on the tail.

15 Open up the base of the neck.

14 Stand up the object with the neck and tail on the bottom. Fold the bases of the wings firmly.

16 Flip over one of the wings to expose the white side of the paper. Turn the lowest part of the neck to the part marked with a red star completely around. Fold the right wing in the same way.

Before flipping over the wings

After flipping over the wings

The neck is viewed from the front.

17 After making firm creases at the edges marked by red stars, close up the base of the neck.

The neck has been closed up.

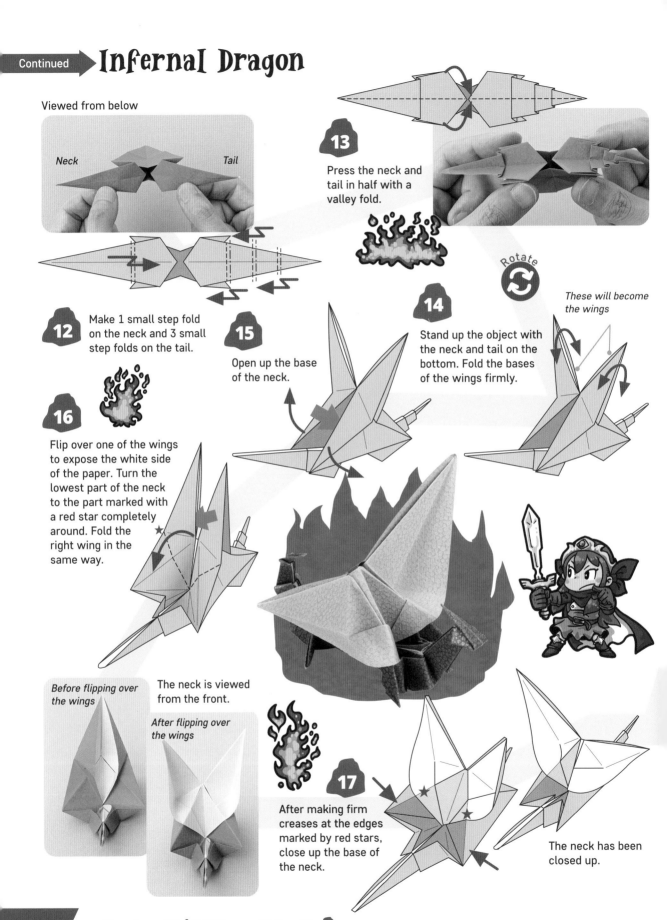

The model has been folded up to step 17.
Does yours look the same?

Viewed from the diagonal front (from the neck side)

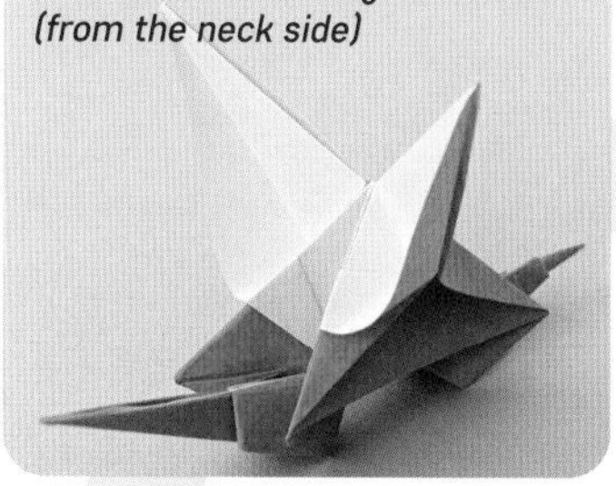

Viewed from the side

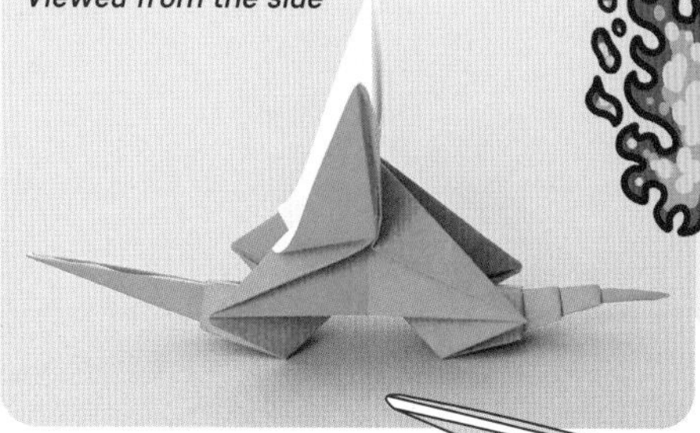

Viewed from the diagonal back (from the tail side)

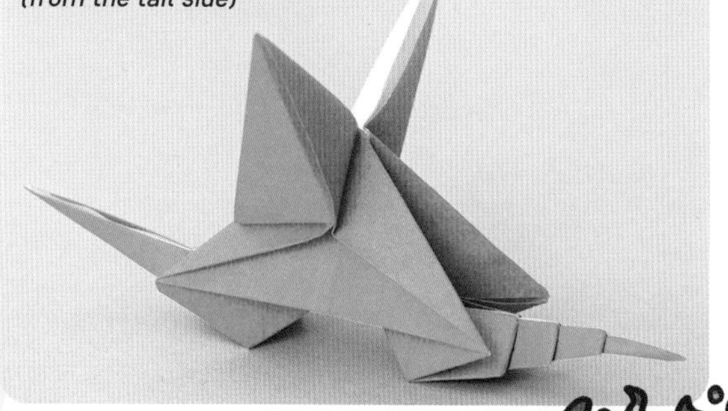

18

Viewed from the side. Fold in the front and back legs.

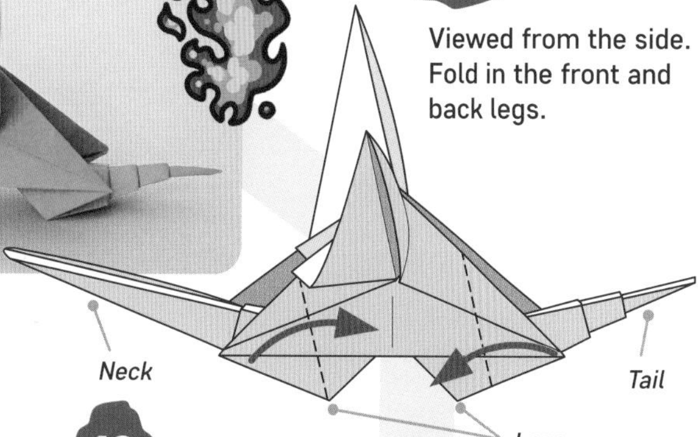

Neck

Tail

Legs

19

Fold up the front leg only. Do the same on the other side.

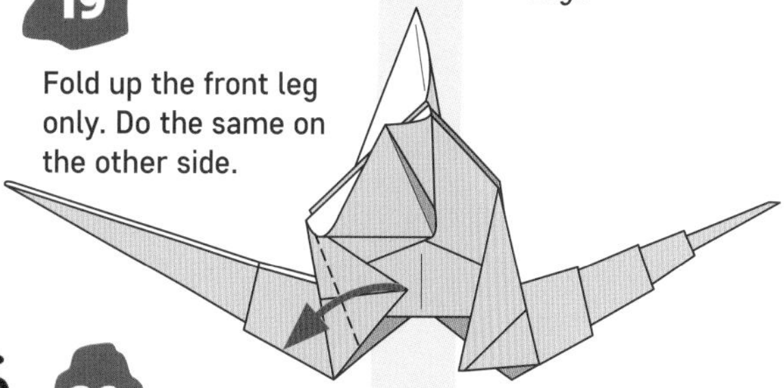

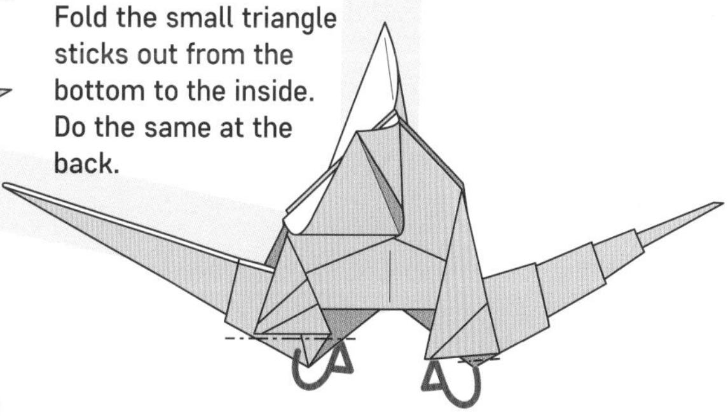

21 Adjust the step folds on the neck and tail a bit to make them curve up.

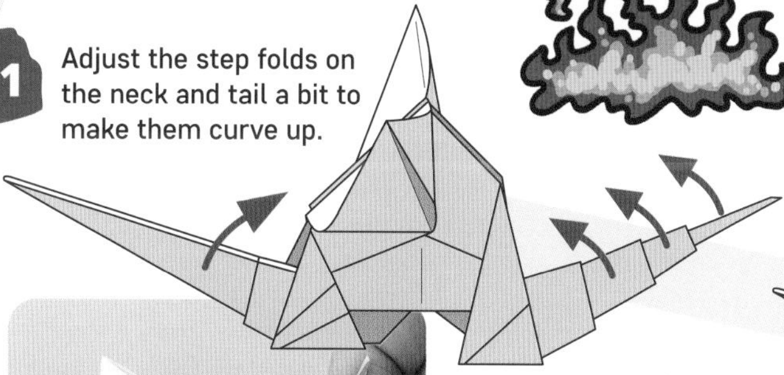

20

Fold the small triangle sticks out from the bottom to the inside. Do the same at the back.

Pinch with your fingers and pull up.

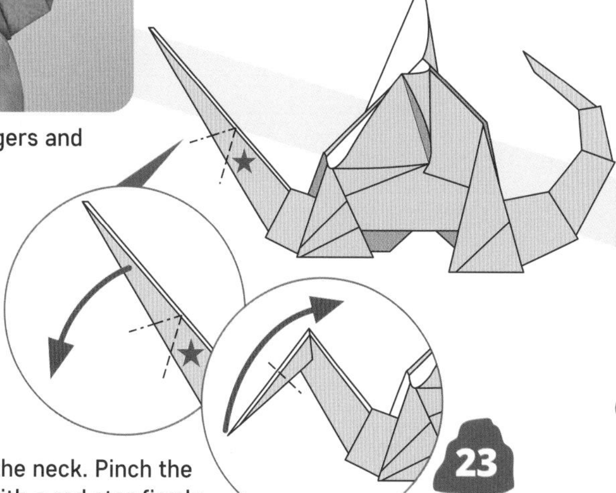

Finished

22

A close-up of the neck. Pinch the part marked with a red star firmly, fold down the tip of the head and make it cover the neck.

23

Fold back to make the horn.

You did well! This is easier to fold if you use a large piece of paper.

Treasure Chest

Most treasure chests contain treasure, but if you're unlucky they may contain monsters. Open it and find out!

Convenience	★ ★ ★
Durability	★ ★ ★ ★ ★
Price	★ ★
Characteristics	Some treasure chests are cursed.

VIDEO
Type this URL into your browser:
tuttlepublishing.com/origami-monsters-and-magic

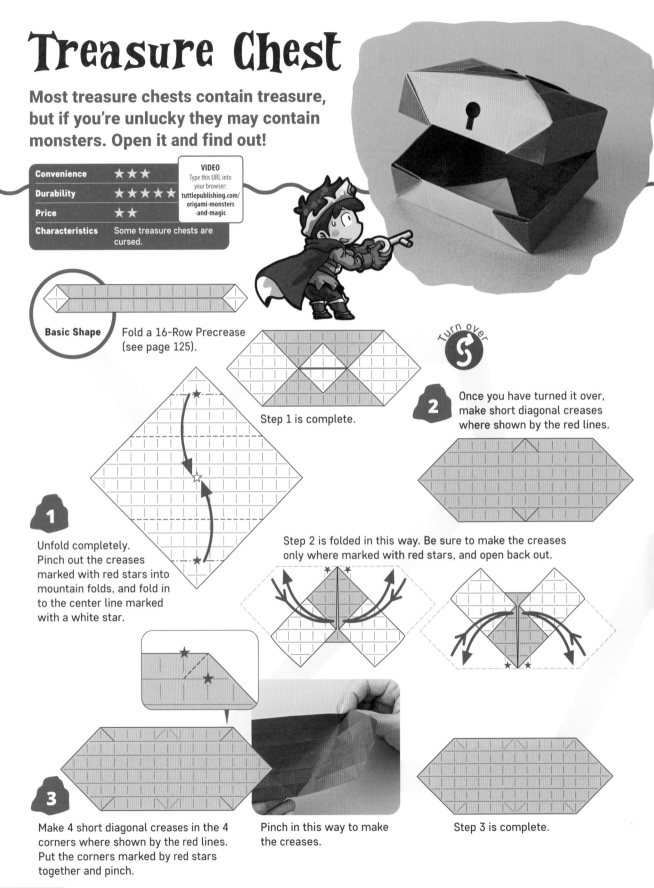

Basic Shape Fold a 16-Row Precrease (see page 125).

Step 1 is complete.

1 Unfold completely. Pinch out the creases marked with red stars into mountain folds, and fold in to the center line marked with a white star.

Turn over

2 Once you have turned it over, make short diagonal creases where shown by the red lines.

Step 2 is folded in this way. Be sure to make the creases only where marked with red stars, and open back out.

3 Make 4 short diagonal creases in the 4 corners where shown by the red lines. Put the corners marked by red stars together and pinch.

Pinch in this way to make the creases.

Step 3 is complete.

In the corresponding video, this is titled "Treasure Box."

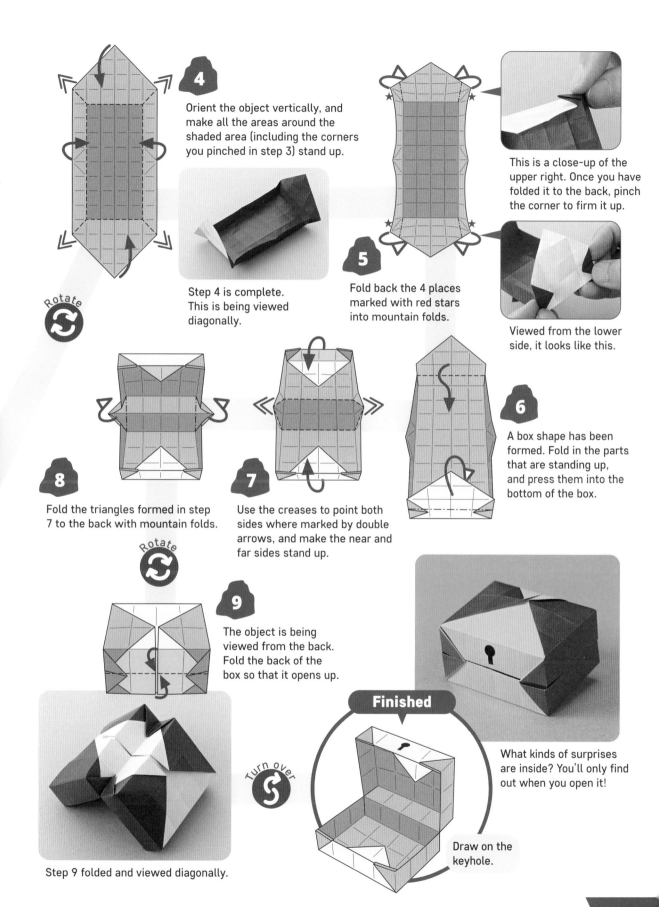

4

Orient the object vertically, and make all the areas around the shaded area (including the corners you pinched in step 3) stand up.

Step 4 is complete. This is being viewed diagonally.

This is a close-up of the upper right. Once you have folded it to the back, pinch the corner to firm it up.

5

Fold back the 4 places marked with red stars into mountain folds.

Viewed from the lower side, it looks like this.

Rotate

8

Fold the triangles formed in step 7 to the back with mountain folds.

7

Use the creases to point both sides where marked by double arrows, and make the near and far sides stand up.

6

A box shape has been formed. Fold in the parts that are standing up, and press them into the bottom of the box.

Rotate

9

The object is being viewed from the back. Fold the back of the box so that it opens up.

Step 9 folded and viewed diagonally.

Turn over

Finished

What kinds of surprises are inside? You'll only find out when you open it!

Draw on the keyhole.

Gemstones

You've found the treasure at last! If you fold these gems with glittery paper, they will sparkle all the more. Congratulations on completing your quest!

Convenience	★★★★★	**VIDEO**
Durability	★★	Type this URL into your browser:
Price	★★★★★	tuttlepublishing.com/origami-monsters-and-magic
Characteristics	All the wealth and honor your heart desires!	

Basic Shape

Fold a Balloon Base (see page 126).

1 Fold the upper layer of the right bottom corner to the left edge. Make sure to make the top edge is horizontally level.

2 Fold the upper layer of the left bottom corner to the red star and open back out to make a crease.

3 Insert the left corner into the pocket as shown.

4 It will form this shape. Fold the back in the same way, following steps 1–3.

5 Fold the top triangle to the back and front to make a crease.

6 Insert your finger into the hole in the bottom, and spread out the right side only to make the object three-dimensional. The left side should remain closed.

The object has been puffed up.

Rotate ↻

Finished

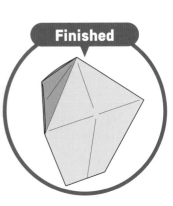

118 **SHOWDOWN IN THE DUNGEON**

In the corresponding video, this is titled "Origami Jewelry."

Now You Are an Origami Hero!

Origami Monsters and Magic
Achievement Checklist

Make a check mark to record the items you have folded. Once you fold them all, you will become the ultimate "Origami Hero!"

In Alphabetical Order

The name of the item.

The "Disappearing" Ghost

✓✓ `4` 78

Darken the checkmark when you have conquered the item. You can write in the achievement date too.

The page the item appears on.

The chapter the item appears in.

Battle Claws
✓✓ `3` 70

Bewitched Wolf
✓✓ `1` 16

Bolt Thrower
✓✓ `3` 62

Cat Familiar
✓✓ `2` 46

Chattering Teeth
✓✓ `5` 104

Creepy Hands
✓✓ `5` 102

Crucifix
✓✓ `4` 92

Deadly Spider
✓✓ `5` 111

"Disappearing" Ghost, the
✓✓ `4` 78

Evil Tree Stump
✓✓ `1` 14

Face of Dracula, the
✓✓ `4` 90

Fake Mustache
✓✓ `4` 96

Fish Bones
✓✓ `1` 28

Flaming Torch
✓✓ `5` 106

How Many Were You Able To Fold?

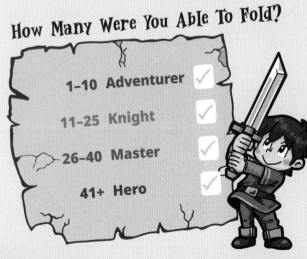

- 1–10 **Adventurer** ✓
- 11–25 **Knight** ✓
- 26–40 **Master** ✓
- 41+ **Hero** ✓

Loch Ness Monster, the
✓✓ | 1 | 34

Flapping Bat
✓✓ | 5 | 108

Magic Lamp
✓✓ | 2 | 42

Flexible Sword
✓✓ | 3 | 60

Magic Wand
✓✓ | 2 | 40

Forest Gnomes
✓✓ | 1 | 22

Magic "House-Key"
✓✓ | 2 | 54

Gemstones
✓✓ | 5 | 118

Magic Soft Serve Ice Cream Cone
✓✓ | 2 | 56

Grim Reaper, the
✓✓ | 4 | 86

Magician's Hat, the
✓✓ | 2 | 38

Haunted Chair
✓✓ | 2 | 55

Mandrake
✓✓ | 2 | 48

Infernal Dragon
✓✓ | 5 | 112

Messenger Owl
✓✓ | 2 | 45

Invincible Shield
✓✓ | 3 | 72

Ninja Star
✓✓ | 3 | 68

Jaw-Dropping Skull
✓✓ | 4 | 82

Noodle-Necked Monster
✓✓ | 4 | 76

Lantern Ghost
✓✓ | 4 | 74

Pecking Bird
✓✓ | 1 | 20

Phoenix

✓✓ | 2 | 52

Pop-Out Eyeballs

✓✓ | 4 | 94

Prehistoric Fish

✓✓ | 1 | 32

Reaper's Scythe

✓✓ | 4 | 88

Riding Broom

✓✓ | 2 | 44

Self-Destruct Button

✓✓ | 3 | 64

Shellfish of Terror

✓✓ | 1 | 30

Squawking Crow

✓✓ | 4 | 89

Tombstone

✓✓ | 4 | 80

Tornado Rabbit

✓✓ | 1 | 18

Toxic Mushrooms

✓✓ | 1 | 21

Treasure Chest

✓✓ | 5 | 116

Unicorn

✓✓ | 2 | 50

Wagging Tongue

✓✓ | 4 | 98

War Hammer

✓✓ | 3 | 66

Werebear, the

✓✓ | 1 | 24

Whispering Imp

✓✓ | 5 | 110

Wobbly Zombie

✓✓ | 4 | 84

Origami Bases

Here's how to fold the origami bases that are used at the beginning of most projects.

Blintz Base

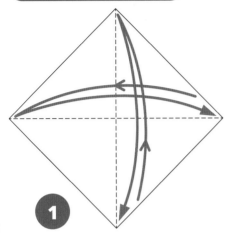

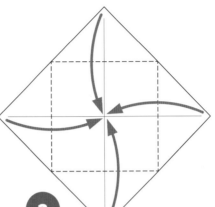

Finished

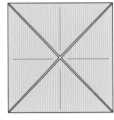

1 Fold the paper in half corner to corner both ways and unfold to make 2 creases.

2 Fold the 4 corners to meet at the center point.

Boat Base

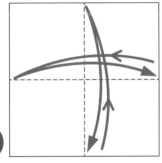

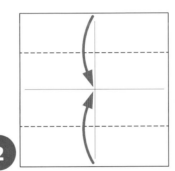

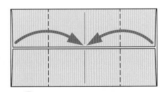

1 Fold the paper in half edge to edge both ways and unfold to make 2 creases.

2 Fold the top and bottom edges to the center line.

3 Fold the left and right edges to the center line.

Finished

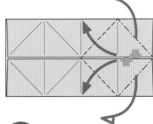

6 The object is being opened up and flattened. Fold the left half in the same way.

5 Insert your fingers where indicated by the squat arrows, and use the creases to open up and middle and flatten.

4 Fold diagonally both ways and unfold to make 2 creases. Unfold the flaps you folded in step 3.

8-Row Precrease (1)

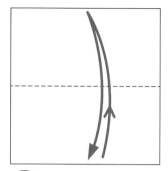

1 Fold the paper in half and unfold to make a crease.

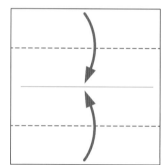

2 Fold the top and bottom edges to the center line.

4 Unfold completely.

Step 3 is complete.

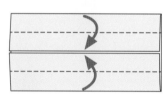

3 Fold the top and bottom edges to the center line again.

Rotate

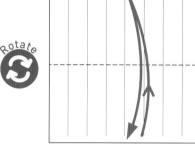

5 Place the paper so that the creases are running vertically, and repeat steps 1–3.

Finished

Although they look similar, when seen from the side, the 8-Row Precrease (1) and 8-Row Precrease (2) are very different.

8-Row Precrease (1)

8-Row Precrease (2)

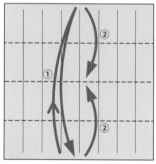

Turn over

Only the upper layer is folded. Creases are not made on the back piece of paper.

1 Follow the directions for 8-Row Precrease (1) up to step 4, and turn the paper over so that the colored side is facing up and the creases are vertical. Fold in half and unfold to make a crease (1), and fold the top and bottom edges to the center line (2).

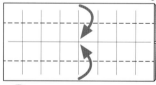

2 Once you turn the paper over, fold in the top and bottom edges to the center line. However, do not fold the paper in the back— leave it unfolded.

8-Row Precrease (2)

Finished

3 Fold the top and bottom edges to the center line.

124

16-Row Precrease

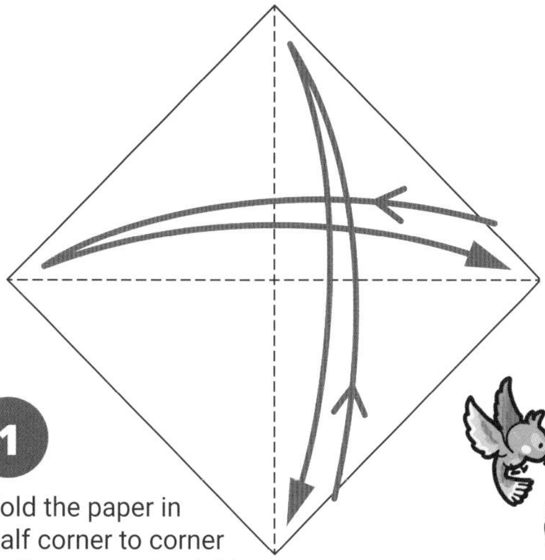

1 Fold the paper in half corner to corner both ways and unfold to make 2 creases.

2 Fold the top and bottom corners to the center point.

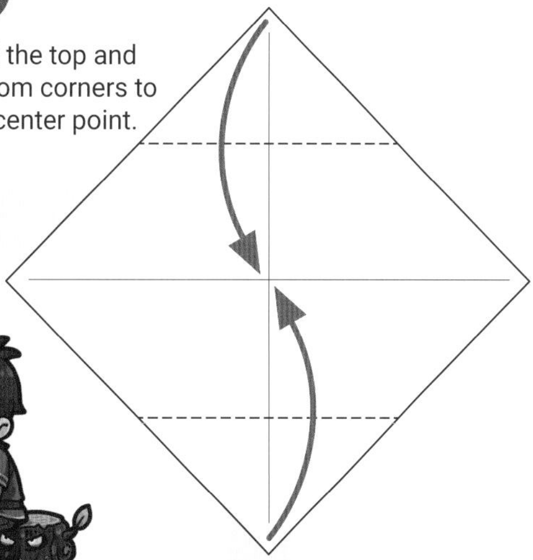

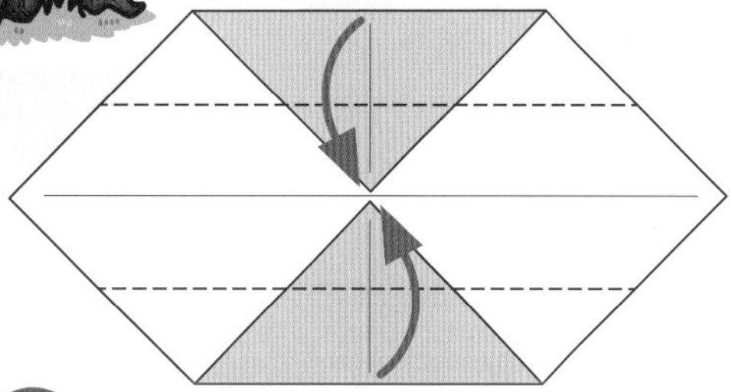

3 Fold the top and bottom edges to the center line.

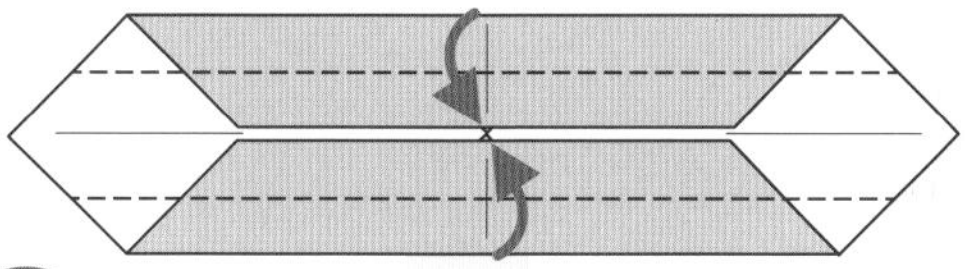

4 Fold the top and bottom edges to the center line once again.

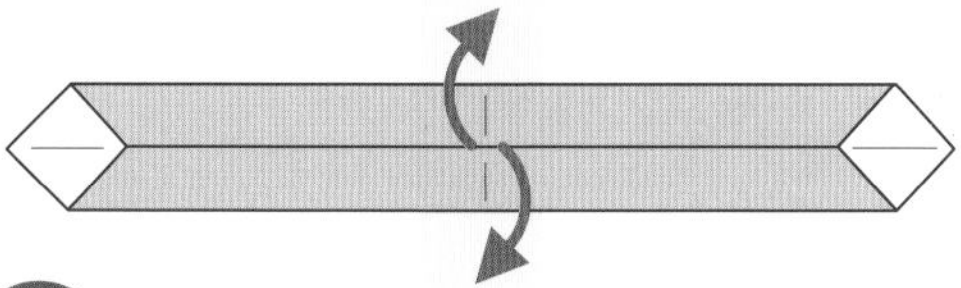

5 Unfold completely.

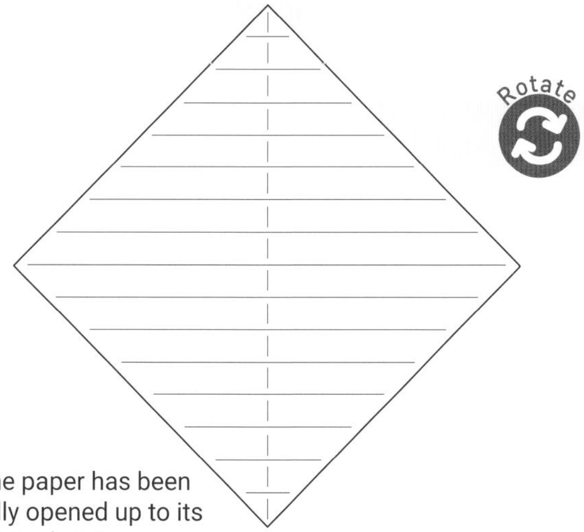

The paper has been fully opened up to its original state.

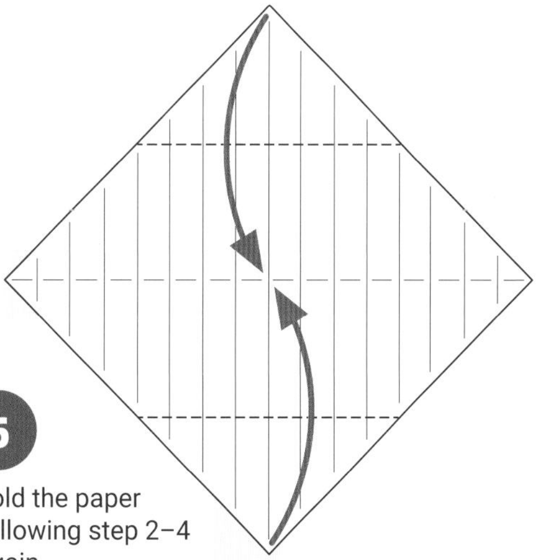

Rotate

6 Fold the paper following step 2–4 again.

Finished

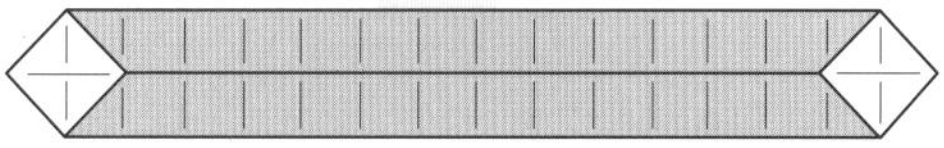

Fish Base

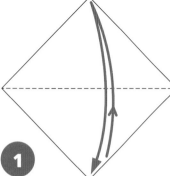

1 Fold the paper in half corner to corner and unfold to make a crease.

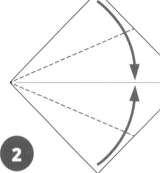

2 Fold the top left and bottom left edges to the center line.

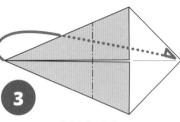

3 Mountain fold the left corner back in half so that it meets the right corner.

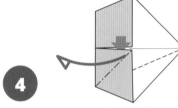

4 Insert your finger where indicated by the squat arrow, open up the corner in the direction of the long arrow and flatten.

5 Fold back and flatten the top half in the same way.

Finished

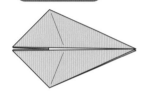

Balloon Base

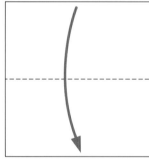

1 Fold in half, top edge to bottom edge.

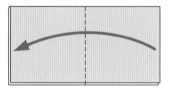

2 Fold in half again.

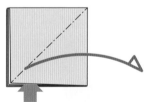

3 Insert your fingers where indicated by the squat arrow, open up the middle in the direction of the long arrow and flatten.

Step 3 is being opened up.

Turn over

4 Once you have turned it over, insert your finger where indicated by the squat arrow, open up the middle in the direction of the long arrow and flatten.

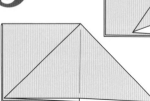

Step 3 has been flattened.

Finished

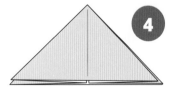

Crane Base

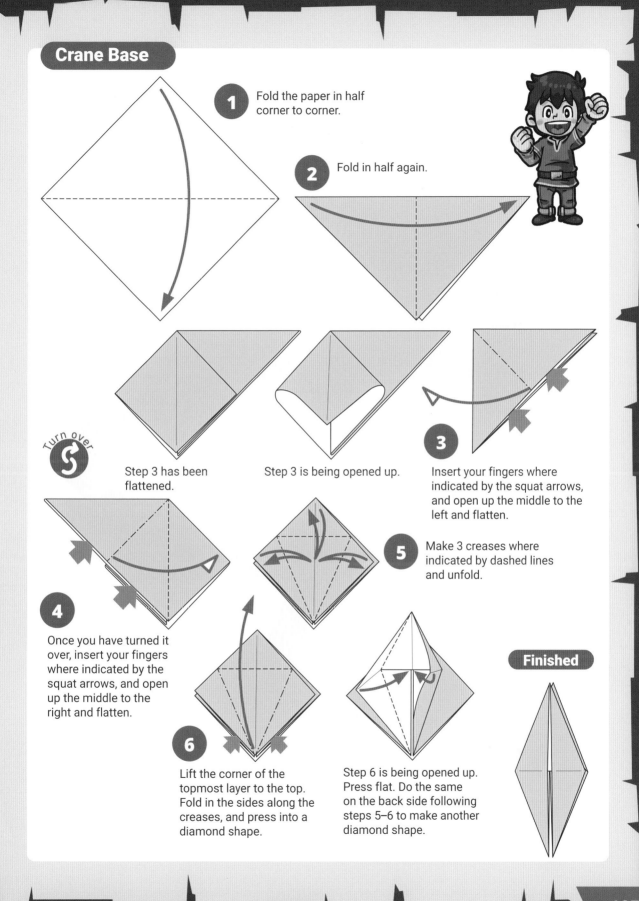

1 Fold the paper in half corner to corner.

2 Fold in half again.

Step 3 has been flattened.

Step 3 is being opened up.

3 Insert your fingers where indicated by the squat arrows, and open up the middle to the left and flatten.

Turn over

4 Once you have turned it over, insert your fingers where indicated by the squat arrows, and open up the middle to the right and flatten.

5 Make 3 creases where indicated by dashed lines and unfold.

6 Lift the corner of the topmost layer to the top. Fold in the sides along the creases, and press into a diamond shape.

Step 6 is being opened up. Press flat. Do the same on the back side following steps 5–6 to make another diamond shape.

Finished

About the Author

Isamu Sasagawa is a Japanese origami artist. He graduated from the College of Art at the University of Tsukuba. While working as a writer for children's programs and animation scripts, he became active as a picture book author. Additionally, as a "hobbyist-engineer," he publishes origami models and other easy crafts made from everyday (but unusual) materials such as mandarin oranges, wet towels and paper cups on YouTube and his blog. He has published several books on the subject of origami.

YouTube (SasaTube)
https://www.youtube.com/c/IsamuSasagawa

Blog
https://ameblo.jp/sasablog

"Books to Span the East and West"

Tuttle Publishing was founded in 1832 in the small New England town of Rutland, Vermont [USA]. Our core values remain as strong today as they were then—to publish best-in-class books which bring people together one page at a time. In 1948, we established a publishing outpost in Japan—and Tuttle is now a leader in publishing English-language books about the arts, languages and cultures of Asia. The world has become a much smaller place today and Asia's economic and cultural influence has grown. Yet the need for meaningful dialogue and information about this diverse region has never been greater. Over the past seven decades, Tuttle has published thousands of books on subjects ranging from martial arts and paper crafts to language learning and literature—and our talented authors, illustrators, designers and photographers have won many prestigious award. We welcome you to explore the wealth of information available on Asia at **www.tuttlepublishing.com**.

Published by Tuttle Publishing, an imprint of Periplus Editions (HK) Ltd

www.tuttlepublishing.com

978-4-8053-1878-2

Yokai to Maho Origami
Copyright © Isamu Sasagawa 2022
English translation rights arranged with
SHUFUNOTOMO CO., LTD.
through Japan UNI Agency, Inc., Tokyo

English translation © 2024 Periplus Editions (HK) Ltd
Translated from Japanese by Makiko Itoh

Printed in China   2407EP
28 27 26 25 24   10 9 8 7 6 5 4 3 2 1

Distributed by

North America, Latin America & Europe
Tuttle Publishing
364 Innovation Drive
North Clarendon,
VT 05759-9436 U.S.A.
Tel: (802) 773-8930
Fax: (802) 773-6993
info@tuttlepublishing.com
www.tuttlepublishing.com

Japan
Tuttle Publishing
Yaekari Building, 3rd Floor
5-4-12 Osaki
Shinagawa-ku
Tokyo 141-0032
Tel: (81) 3 5437-0171
Fax: (81) 3 5437-0755
sales@tuttle.co.jp
www.tuttle.co.jp

Asia Pacific
Berkeley Books Pte. Ltd.
3 Kallang Sector #04-01
Singapore 349278
Tel: (65) 6741-2178
Fax: (65) 6741-2179
inquiries@periplus.com.sg
www.tuttlepublishing.com